The Taming of Scarcity and the Problems of Plenty
Rethinking International Relations and American Grand Strategy in a New Era

Francis J. Gavin

'Francis J. Gavin's marvellous essay describes the most fundamental shift in international relations since the advent of the modern state system: from an international politics of inter-state competition in the face of scarcity, to a global order defined by "problems of plenty". Not only does Gavin show that these latter challenges are more pressing, more threatening and more existentially risky than traditional geopolitical challenges, he also persuasively argues that the international institutional architecture that was built to manage inter-state competition is fundamentally inadequate for managing the problems of plenty. He concludes with a bracing call for a revision to American grand strategy based on promoting a new geopolitics of positive-sum planetary cooperation.'

Nils Gilman, Senior Vice President of Programs, Berggruen Institute; Deputy Editor of Noema Magazine

'Francis J. Gavin tells an original and compelling story of how tectonic shifts in demography, health, information and international institutions, along with the increasing costs of great-power war, have all combined to move international politics away from scarcity to the new problems of plenty. But we risk disaster if our leaders continue to maintain outdated mindsets and strategies. An essential read for anyone who wants to understand the strategic imperatives of today – and tomorrow.'

Professor Janice Gross Stein, University Professor, Belzberg Professor of Conflict Management and Founding Director, Munk School of Global Affairs and Public Policy, University of Toronto

The Taming of Scarcity and the Problems of Plenty
Rethinking International Relations and American Grand Strategy in a New Era

Francis J. Gavin

IISS The International Institute for Strategic Studies

The International Institute for Strategic Studies

Arundel House | 6 Temple Place | London | WC2R 2PG | UK

First published March 2024 by **Routledge**
4 Park Square, Milton Park, Abingdon, Oxon, OX14 4RN

for **The International Institute for Strategic Studies**
Arundel House, 6 Temple Place, London, WC2R 2PG, UK
www.iiss.org

Simultaneously published in the USA and Canada by **Routledge**
52 Vanderbilt Avenue, New York, NY 10017

Routledge is an imprint of Taylor & Francis, an Informa Business

© 2024 The International Institute for Strategic Studies

DIRECTOR-GENERAL AND CHIEF EXECUTIVE Dr Bastian Giegerich
SERIES EDITOR Dr Benjamin Rhode
ASSOCIATE EDITOR Alice Aveson
EDITORIAL Gregory Brooks, Jill Lally, Michael Marsden, Nicholas Woodroof
PRODUCTION Alessandra Beluffi, Ravi Gopar, Jade Panganiban, James Parker, Kelly Verity
COVER ARTWORK Adapted from advertisements published in the United States during the Second
World War. The IISS is grateful to Revere Copper Products Inc. for its permission to adapt these
original images.

The International Institute for Strategic Studies is an independent centre for research, information
and debate on the problems of conflict, however caused, that have, or potentially have, an important
military content. The Council and Staff of the Institute are international and its membership is
drawn from almost 100 countries. The Institute is independent and it alone decides what activities
to conduct. It owes no allegiance to any government, any group of governments or any political or
other organisation. The IISS stresses rigorous research with a forward-looking policy orientation
and places particular emphasis on bringing new perspectives to the strategic debate.

The Institute's publications are designed to meet the needs of a wider audience than its own
membership and are available on subscription, by mail order and in good bookshops. Further details
at www.iiss.org.

British Library Cataloguing in Publication Data
A catalogue record for this book is available from the British Library

Library of Congress Cataloging in Publication Data

ADELPHI series
ISSN 1944-5571

ADELPHI AP502–504
ISBN 978-1-032-80557-3 / eB 978-1-003-49743-1

Contents

Note from the Series Editor   6
Author   7
Acknowledgements   8

The Taming of Scarcity and the Problems of Plenty   9
Introduction   9

I. War and conquest in the age of scarcity   21
II. The taming of scarcity and the end of empire   33
III. The problems of plenty   49
IV. Unspoken assumptions, time lags and historical anamnesis   62
V. American grand strategy in a world of plenty   74

Conclusion   88

Notes   97

NOTE FROM THE SERIES EDITOR

Since its inception more than 60 years ago, the *Adelphi* Series has represented the Institute's flagship contribution to policy-relevant, original academic research. For much of its history, the Series took the form of the *Adelphi Papers*: pithy publications longer than a journal article but shorter than a full-length book. The *Papers* are remembered fondly by their many readers over the decades and continue to be consulted today, prized for their crisp analytic judgements and concise prose.

In 2010, the Series evolved into short books, typically around 40,000 words long. These 'non-fiction novellas', in the phrase of our Executive Chairman Sir John Chipman KCMG, could now be made available to a broader audience while maintaining the analytic punch of their predecessors. This newer format has served us well and we intend to maintain it. But there have been times when we have considered whether a shorter product, closer to the length of the old *Adelphi Papers*, could perhaps be more suitable for addressing particular questions.

This stimulating and concise volume by Professor Francis J. Gavin is the first in a number of shorter *Adelphi* books – closer in length to the original *Papers* and therefore perhaps nearer in form to an extended essay than a novella – which will appear in the Series. We will publish them occasionally, when appropriate.

We hope that you enjoy this first appearance of an *Adelphi* book in a new but pleasantly familiar format.

Dr Benjamin Rhode
Senior Fellow, IISS
Editor, The *Adelphi* Series
January 2024

Francis J. Gavin is the Giovanni Agnelli Distinguished Professor and the inaugural Director of the Henry A. Kissinger Center for Global Affairs at Johns Hopkins School of Advanced International Studies. Previously, he was the first Frank Stanton Chair in Nuclear Security Policy Studies at Massachusetts Institute of Technology (MIT) and the Tom Slick Professor of International Affairs and the Director of the Robert S. Strauss Center for International Security and Law at the University of Texas.

Gavin earned his BA at the University of Chicago in Political Science, an MSt from the University of Oxford in Modern European History and a PhD in history from the University of Pennsylvania.

He has been a National Security Fellow at the Olin Institute, Harvard University, an International Security Fellow at the Belfer Center for Science and International Affairs, Harvard University, a Donald Harrington Faculty Fellow at the University of Texas, a Smith Richardson Junior Faculty Fellow, a Senior Research Fellow at the Nobel Institute, Oslo, Norway, a Public Policy Fellow at the Wilson Center, and the Ernest May Senior Visiting Professor in Applied History, John F. Kennedy School of Government, Harvard University. From 2005 to 2010, he directed the American Assembly's multi-year, national initiative, 'The Next Generation Project: U.S. Global Policy and the Future of International Institutions'.

Gavin currently serves on the CIA Historical Panel and is a lifetime member of the Council on Foreign Relations. He is the founding Chair of the Editorial Board for the *Texas National Security Review*.

Gavin's writings include *Gold, Dollars, and Power: The Politics of International Monetary Relations, 1958–1971* (University of North Carolina Press), *Nuclear Statecraft: History and Strategy in America's Atomic Age* (Cornell University Press) and *Nuclear Weapons and American Grand Strategy* (Brookings Institution Press), which was named a 2020 Choice Outstanding Academic Title. His book *Thinking Historically: A Guide to Statecraft and Strategy* (Yale University Press) is forthcoming.

ACKNOWLEDGEMENTS

A much different version of this essay was originally sponsored by the Office of Net Assessment in the US Department of Defense. I am grateful for their support and the comments from James Baker, David Epstein and Caroline Pestel. I am also grateful for the comments received during presentations for the 'Japan, US, and the Future of World Order' meeting, the Nuclear Studies Research Initiative meeting at Nemacolin, the International Relations and Foreign Policy Seminar at the John Sloan Dickey Center for International Understanding, Dartmouth University, a 'murder board' organised at the Henry A. Kissinger Center for Global Affairs, as well as especially insightful suggestions and support from Benjamin Rhode and Dana Allin at the IISS. Julie Beckenstein, William Ellison, Jonathan Esty and Tristan Gutbezahl provided outstanding research assistantship. I have been very fortunate that far too many people to name encouraged this project, but I am especially thankful to Natalie Britton, Jim Steinberg, Hal Brands and Joshua Rovner.

The Taming of Scarcity and the Problems of Plenty

Introduction

Man living in 'the state of nature' provides a powerful analogy for understanding the international system. Many experts on global politics have long based their world views on the insights of the English philosopher Thomas Hobbes (1588–1679), who suggested that this condition generates a war of all against all, as individuals struggle to escape the disorder and dangers of anarchy in a world of mistrust and scarcity.

What are the characteristics of the state of nature, and do they explain the international system? Imagine two different shipwrecks. The first shipwrecked crew ends up on a desert island with little edible food or easily accessed shelter, buffeted by volatile weather. The crew must compete, often viciously, to obtain the basic but scarce resources needed to sustain life. To stay alive and to marshal limited food-producing land and housing, they understand they must escape anarchy and establish order. But in a situation marked by scarcity and deep distrust, cooperation and generosity go unrewarded and collective action is nearly impossible. Predation is the rule, and imposing order on the island is coercive, bloody and non-consensual. Controlling fellow inhabitants and the limited usable land is the key to power, survival and success. The Hobbesian dynamics of this island are familiar to many analysts of geopolitics, order and international relations.

Now picture a different island, in a more temperate zone – a treasure island. Food and natural shelter are plentiful and there is space for all the shipwrecked crew.[1] The island inhabitants feel freer to share information and trade with each other. In time, however, a problem develops. Piles of recklessly discarded half-eaten food – fruit or the carcasses of easily captured, abundant animals – attract mosquitoes carrying a potentially lethal disease. Unlike the desert island, the treasure island is threatened less by a challenge brought by scarcity than a problem emerging from plenty.

Solving this challenge brought about by abundance requires that the residents of the treasure island cooperate on waste disposal. This is not easy – collective action is just as hard as on the desert island, and order-building remains difficult. The islanders are obsessed with who possesses more land and wealth, and few people want to sacrifice their individual habits and preferences for the common good. Individuals are tempted to threaten coercion and violence, though they soon realise that this does little to solve their most pressing problems. In the end, however, the inhabitants of the treasure island recognise that they can only survive if they reward those who develop the most innovative solutions and design mechanisms that attract consensus and establish fair, effective and enforceable rules to mitigate a potentially existential threat.

These examples show that nature and its 'state' is diverse, and divergent landscapes demand different responses for humans to survive and thrive. Nor is nature static: as any ecologist knows, habitats evolve over time, often in mysterious and transformative ways, shifting the incentives and behaviours of those living within them. Human choices also markedly alter these environments, depending on how political, social and economic order is established.

In the long run, neither island setting is necessarily safer than the other: the inhabitants of both face existential threats and collective-action problems. And many things can spark violence, organised or otherwise: the residents of either island may be as likely to be murdered in their sleep because of a quarrel over honour, a misunderstanding or a romance gone awry. While food and shelter are abundant on the treasure island, jealousies about who has more – in other words, concerns over relative gains – may intensify in this world of plenty. The characteristics of nature on each island, however, incentivise different political behaviours and order-building choices to achieve safety and success. The strategies that generate stability, prosperity and security on one island may bring disaster for the other. Self-help on one island, in other words, is suicide on the other.

Might the same be true for the international system?

Like nature, the international system is not static. This essay will argue that the underlying structure, incentives and costs shaping international relations, state behaviour and the nature of power are profoundly different today to how they were in the past, in ways that are scarcely recognised and widely misunderstood. For much of history, world politics was similar to the desert island, with states, leaders and their populations tormented by scarcity. For most people, life was as Hobbes had described the state of nature: 'nasty, brutish, and short'. As a result, the nation-states and empires best able to organise their economies, societies and politics to conquer territory and control populations, near and far – if only to avoid being conquered and exploited themselves – were those that thrived.

This process intensified during the late industrial age, particularly in modern Europe. Dramatic increases in population fuelled Malthusian and social Darwinian fears that without markets, colonies and pre-eminent offensive military strength to control more territory and populations, competing states and empires would be unable to access basic resources like food and fuel, or markets, putting their survival at risk. As a result, Western states organised, mobilised for and unleashed unprecedented levels of imperial conquest, murderous war and revolutionary disruption that killed tens of millions of people worldwide in the first half of the twentieth century.

Even as the world was riven by these catastrophic conflicts, however, the international system was in the process of being transformed, and with it, how national interest should be assessed and power defined. Five tectonic shifts were particularly consequential. Firstly, an unexpected and voluntary demographic compression unfolded in the developed world, with birth rates falling precipitously; as median ages increased and population growth slowed, objective pressures for conquest decreased. Secondly, an economic–technological revolution emerged that massively improved agricultural yields and the availability of food, dramatically boosted industrial productivity and transformed finance capitalism, while improving housing and health, and making accessible, affordable fuel bountiful. Thirdly, an information revolution took place, whereby increased literacy and technological change dramatically expanded the amount of and access to knowledge about the world. Fourthly, leaders of the developed world created domestic and international governing institutions and practices, which, amongst other benefits, generated greater domestic stability and socio-economic well-being, eliminated great depressions, and provided personal as well as collective security, creating a global order that prized and worked to protect sovereignty and, in time, human rights. Finally, groundbreaking new military capabilities, especially thermonuclear weapons, prohibitively increased the costs and risks of great-power wars of conquest.

These revolutions combined to reduce the long shadow of famine, disease and misery that had long fallen upon the human experience, while massively increasing total wealth and information, and weakening core drivers of conflict, therefore immeasurably improving quality of life in the developed world. As population growth has flattened and populations have aged, food, resources and markets have become more abundant, and disintermediated flows of information have exploded. Both the cost of and the decreased pay-off from conquest have made the idea of fully mobilised, total wars of empire increasingly illogical and self-defeating. The nuclear revolution and transformations in national and global governance have amplified these effects. As a result, knowledge, technology and innovation have increasingly replaced land as a primary source of wealth, prestige and power, and the tools of attraction have became more effective than coercion.

This is no Whig version of international relations, however, nor does this essay suggest, as Norman Angell did before the First World War, that the logic of trade, finance and interdependence should generate lasting peace and stability.[2] Other causes of conflict and violence persist. Wars, once started, can develop their own terrifying logic. Scarcity still afflicts low-income countries, and corners of high-income ones. Time lags, unspoken assumptions and what this essay labels 'historical anamnesis' – the inability to properly recognise and accept when circumstances are improving – often cause the leading powers to act against their own interests and the incentives of the international system, behaving as if scarcity were still the norm. By remaining trapped in the past, great powers increasingly misunderstand or mischaracterise what the historian Adam Tooze and others have called the global 'polycrisis' – multiple crises converging, interacting and amplifying each other.[3]

One set of crises, however, looms above the rest. The developed world's success over scarcity has generated fresh dangers, which I label the 'problems of plenty'. Since the end of the Second World War, a remarkable age of abundance in the developed world has generated previously unimaginable wealth, increased security from conquest and allowed for vast knowledge of the world. This process, however, has also transformed the international system into one that more resembles the treasure island. The current world order produces great material output, generated by increasing global exchange, but distributing it amongst and between populations is contentious. This enormous prosperity has spawned the grave risks of climate, ecological, migratory and public-health catastrophes. The emergence of new technologies, developed largely in the private sector, has solved innumerable problems, while also creating frightening new ones. Surprisingly, an unlimited amount of data and information, no longer intermediated by legacy institutions, generates different though equally fraught dangers as scarce information controlled by religious institutions or the state. The age of abundance has promoted tolerance and radical individuality, while undermining social cohesion and weakening any sense of common purpose. Governing norms and institutions developed for a different era have been exposed as ill-suited to contemporary problems, generating a crisis of political legitimacy while stoking polarisation. The problems of plenty are fostering planetary risks and dangers as concerning as, if not more than, the imperial wars that plagued world politics during the age of scarcity, threatening disaster and even risking a return to the brutal conflict, disruption and scarcity of earlier periods.

Since the end of the Cold War, explanations of the nature of the international system and identification of the best grand strategies to navigate it have been fiercely contested. The terms of the debate, however – liberalism vs realism, primacy vs restraint, civilisational factors, even terms such as 'geopolitics', 'great-power politics' and 'Cold War II' – risk missing the fundamental drivers, dynamics and dangers of the current and future world. The most popular theories of world politics are rooted in a logic of scarcity that no longer applies, while decision-makers pursue policies in ways that were appropriate in the past but are potentially ruinous to the effort to meet the current challenges of plenty.

Indeed, the institutions, practices, theories and policies that helped explain and largely tamed the world of scarcity by generating massive wealth and undertaking punishing conquest are often unsuitable for addressing the problems of plenty. The very image of state power – a centralised bureaucratic government, mobilising a unified national society and converting its mass industrial economic capabilities into offensive military capability to territorially expand – is largely misplaced to meet these new planetary challenges. To be clear, this does not mean that military power will disappear as a key feature of international relations, or that other causes of conflict – concerns over reputation and status, long-running territorial and political disputes, regional tensions, terrorism, the need to protect global norms or states acting against their own material interests – will not persist. While war will not disappear, however, the planetary threats brought by plenty are more pressing, more threatening, indeed, more existential than the traditional geopolitical challenges that currently dominate both academic and policy discussions. New conceptual lenses, innovative policies and processes, and transformed institutions will be essential for confronting and solving the problems of plenty, without undermining the expanding efforts against scarcity.

Caveats and road map

This essay offers three key arguments. Firstly, while war has been a persistent, deadly part of the human experience – and will remain so in the future – its shape, course, causes and frequency have changed dramatically over time, generated by an evolving mix of individual, local and structural forces. Scarcity and fears of future scarcity in basic economic resources, information and security make conflict both more likely and more deadly. A particularly murderous and aggressive form of imperial war and conquest emerged during the late industrial age, from the final decades of the nineteenth century to the middle of the twentieth, first in Europe and then globally. This expansive imperial conquest, ideological fervour and global war were driven in large measure by historically unique and ultimately transitory systemic pressures related to scarcity and fears of future scarcity. Secondly, over the past three-quarters of a century, the developed world has largely tamed scarcity, generating unimaginable abundance, technological change, increased security and sociocultural transformation, albeit unevenly, while avoiding the kinds of imperial, great-power wars of conquest that plagued world politics in the past. As a result, the drive for empire and conquest has faded, and the things that constitute power and national interest have been transformed. Today's international system is shaped by new and potentially existential dangers – the problems of plenty – that are nothing like those of past centuries. Misunderstanding these challenges risks catastrophe. Thirdly, the institutions, policies and conceptual lenses developed in the age of scarcity are ill-suited to meet the potentially catastrophic challenges of the era of plenty.

A few caveats are in order. Any effort to describe and assess the evolving nature of the international system over centuries and continents is bound to do violence to historical nuance, specific circumstances and context, while generating many exceptions to the larger argument. People faced ruinous climate disasters, pandemics and technological disruptions in past centuries, while avoiding total war for decades at a time. Conflict and war – even the threat of great-power war – will likely remain consequential factors in world politics. It can often be difficult to distinguish between problems of scarcity and plenty. At times, plenty and scarcity persist less as opposites, rather coexisting and feeding into each other, while at other times, the dangers caused by plenty threaten to return many parts of the world to the conditions of scarcity. Scholars and analysts engage in deep, contested arguments about many of the contentions below, which deserve far greater exploration than the space available allows.

Furthermore, fixing the historical timeline and causal arrows for the transition from scarcity to plenty is not always clear-cut, for at least three reasons. Firstly, this transition in the developed world was not sudden, like a lamp immediately illuminating a darkened room. The changes – including increases in food and energy production; demographic compression; improvements in sanitation, education, medicine and public health; the rise of tolerance and the rights revolution; better governance; greater personal, communal and global security; the thermonuclear and satellite revolutions; and the surge in the production and dissemination of information – unfolded at different times and over different intervals, appearing, on occasion, erratically, and at other times suddenly and explosively. And like scarcity, different strands of plenty generated interactive, cumulative and even exponential effects, boosting the consequences of abundance. Secondly, the emergence and consequences of plenty are typically only recognised in retrospect, after long time lags, if they are understood at all. Thirdly, scarcity still affects large parts of the globe. In other parts of the world, only some aspects of plenty have taken root. There is no guarantee that scarcity will not return to the developed world, or that the scarcity that marks the low-income world will not generate conflicts that pull the developed world in.

Critics might reasonably ask: do Russia's brutal invasion of Ukraine and China's threats over Taiwan not demonstrate that great-power conflict has not disappeared? This is an important question, which will be discussed further below. Two points are worth stating in advance. Firstly, Russia's behaviour, along with the United States' disastrous post-9/11 wars in the Middle East, are the exceptions that prove the rule, revealing that invading and trying to occupy sovereign countries, even weaker ones, is often self-defeating in the age of plenty. Secondly, it is important to recognise that there are disparate causes of war. In particular, we must distinguish between irredentism – the finite desire of a state to reclaim territory it believes it has lost – and imperial conquest – an expansive, often unlimited impulse to continue to add territory and empire, a behaviour that marked the age of scarcity. While they may seem similar, they are driven by significantly different factors and forces and demand different grand-strategic responses. Whether China's threatening behaviour towards Taiwan and its neighbours is motivated by irredentism – as is suggested below – or, as many believe, expansive imperialism, is a critical question.

This brings up a second important question: was the taming of scarcity and the rise of plenty driven by structural forces or state choices? It is true that many of the tectonic forces described in the pages that follow, which transformed human life and with it the international system, had little to do with grand strategy in a narrow sense, with many beginning before the Second World War, if not earlier. Identifying deep structural forces does not absolve states, and especially leading powers, from consequential, critical choices; quite the contrary. Sometimes global actors will be able to change, reroute or mitigate powerful underlying forces, whereas at other times they will need to anticipate, adapt and adjust. The key is to recognise and frame the challenges and choices brought by plenty. Pursuing grand strategy as if the world were still shaped by the forces of scarcity risks the kind of catastrophic missteps that could plunge the world into world war while accelerating existential planetary risks that could doom humanity.

The book proceeds as follows: the first section will focus on the past. 'War and conquest in the age of scarcity' will outline the profoundly varied circumstances that shaped human life and explore how, in this world of scarcity, these factors often drove great-power wars of conquest. It will also highlight how the unique but toxic combination of European industrialisation, social Darwinism and Malthusian population fears helped usher in decades of imperialism, world war and deadly revolution between the late nineteenth and mid-twentieth centuries. The second section will assess how the present world came to be. 'The taming of scarcity and the end of empire' will chronicle the profound structural changes and policy choices that ameliorated the pressures of scarcity over the last three-quarters of a century, altered human life and transformed international relations, dampening many of the drivers of imperial conquest and global war. The third section – 'The problems of plenty' – will detail how the reduction of scarcity tragically produced the planetary challenges that threaten the future of international relations and humanity. Five categories of potentially catastrophic challenges emerge from there being 'too much', as opposed to 'too little': production, transmission, information and communication, identity and choice, and expectations. The fourth section – 'Unspoken assumptions, time lags and historical anamnesis' – will explore why these profound changes in the international system and the nature of power are often ignored or misunderstood while they are unfolding, and explain phenomena that appear to contradict the thesis, like Russia's invasion of Ukraine and the increasing tensions and risk of war between China and the US.

What grand strategy should the most important player in the international system, the US, develop to meet the challenges of plenty? Exploring this question will be the focus of the fifth section, 'American grand strategy in a world of plenty'. There are obvious reasons to be sceptical, even wary of America's role. Many of the problems of plenty possess structural roots and are insensitive to traditional policy interventions. The United States' politics are deeply polarised, and some believe it is a declining power. Its often-failed efforts regarding climate change, COVID-19, technology and inequality arguably offer little promise, particularly as its behaviours and policies have been a leading cause of the problems of plenty. There is, however, another perspective. The US, in unexpected ways given its history, helped shape a post-1945 global order that contributed to taming scarcity and accelerating plenty. It also possesses important qualities, ranging from innovation and resilience to adaptability and cultural appeal, which were luxury attributes in a world of scarcity but may provide advantages in tackling the problems of plenty.

If the US is to successfully construct grand strategies and lead a worldwide effort to tame the problems of plenty, it will face difficult choices. It must reorient its policies, conceptual frameworks and institutions to deal with these complex issues, without abandoning the more beneficial aspects of an international order that helped mitigate scarcity. Indeed, it should work to spread the benefits of abundance more widely and fairly, while at the same time identifying and reforming those practices and policies that fuel the problems of plenty. This will not be easy, as much of the institutional architecture built to tame scarcity helped create and accelerate these challenges. Nor can the US resolve the problems of plenty alone. Powerful new actors from the private and non-governmental sectors must be engaged. To deal with these planetary challenges, US leaders will have to increasingly harness the powers of attraction, collaboration and innovation – tools that will be far more effective than leveraging its considerable tools of coercion and violence.

I. War and conquest in the age of scarcity

The current international system is plagued by threats – the problems of plenty – that are unlike those of the past and are likely to get far worse in the years ahead. Before exploring those challenges, however, it is important to understand how dramatically different both the human condition and international relations were in the age of scarcity. It is easy to forget just how dire conditions could be in the not-so-distant past. Human life before the recent age was often marked by misery, violence and uncertainty. The average life expectancy at birth in Europe in 1770 was 34 years. Even by 1900, after decades of industrialisation, it was only 42.7, while the worldwide average was only 32, rising to just 46.5 by 1950. Today, a European can expect to live to nearly 80, a remarkable change, while in the rest of the world life expectancy has reached 71.[4] Even in Burundi, Africa's poorest country, life expectancy has increased from 47 to almost 62 over the last quarter of a century.[5] In 1820, global literacy was estimated to be 12%, whereas today it approaches 90%.[6] Per capita caloric consumption was 13% higher in 2019 than in 1990, and significantly higher than it was in the mid-eighteenth century.[7] To give just one of many examples of disasters that scarcity regularly visited upon the world, in the last 25 years of the nineteenth century, between 30 and 60 million people in Brazil, China and India died of famine.[8] London, one of the wealthiest cities in the world, still had an infant-mortality rate of 16% at the start of the twentieth century.[9] The murder rate in Puritan and Quaker early America was at least four times higher than it is today, and one in ten Americans suffered from syphilis in the 1930s, with devastating consequences.[10] There are countless other measures and stories that detail how much more precarious and miserable life could be in earlier times.

These statistics, stark as they are, cannot completely capture the deep instability and unpredictability of life for most people, most of the time, that persisted until quite recently. Crop failures, famine and disease, fires and floods, financial panics, riots, mass killings and pogroms, slumps, depressions and a general lack of information about the wider world haunted humanity. Intolerance was the norm, and how, where and with whom one lived was determined by the community into which one was born. Government was, for most people in many places, unresponsive, exploitative and even malign. Personal and communal violence were far more persistent, criminal justice rare, and war and the threat of war and its consequences constant. As the great historian of global history William McNeill argued, 'a human life unaffected by famine, pestilence, and war was rare indeed'.[11]

Writ large, this world of misery, violence and unpredictability was shaped by extreme scarcity in at least three broad categories: economics and resources, information, and security.

First and most obvious was economic scarcity. Before the middle of the twentieth century, most of the world, much of the time, worried about access to predictable, stable resources to maintain life. Acquiring clean water, safe housing and enough food consumed much time and effort. Many variables could affect food production, from erratic weather, depleted soil, widespread and untreated disease outbreaks within and between animal herds and crops, to the capricious demands landowners made on the many people who toiled on their land. Food could not be stored for long and spoiled easily, and even when it was available, it was nutritionally unvaried, lacking in the kinds of proteins, fats and vitamins that provided energy and warded off sickness. Disease and famine lurked everywhere, and effective, safe medicine was rare. Housing was scarce and expensive; what machines that existed were rudimentary; and fuel, when it was accessible – largely timber, then coal – was also expensive.

For agrarian workers, however, at least food and fuel were proximate. In many cities, employment, when offered, was often irregular, low-paying and dangerous. Most urban workers, in Europe and elsewhere, were even more vulnerable to famine and, being tightly packed into often unsatisfactory housing, exposed to numerous diseases and sickness. Markets – either for agricultural or industrial goods – were unpredictable and burdened by the difficulties and expense of trade, not the least of which was transport. Financing was constrained and available to few.

The second form of scarcity was informational. The overwhelming majority of people living in centuries past were illiterate. Even those who possessed a basic education could not easily access information about the world. A deep understanding of many subjects needed to survive and thrive – from hygiene, nutrition, medicine and public health to how climate and weather functioned – was absent. Books were scarce, expensive to produce and disseminate, and often unreliable, while newspapers and pamphlets were less scarce but even more error-prone. Knowledge about how the natural and physical world functioned was limited and not widespread, as were social, economic and political knowledge.

The third type of scarcity was security. Crime and violence were far more prevalent, equitable justice rare, mob violence, ethnic cleansing and brutal state repression not uncommon. Political entities, be they nation-states, empires or other polities, often possessed little knowledge of their subjects and limited capabilities (and interest) in protecting them from the vicissitudes of life by providing jobs and opportunities, education, healthcare, or secure and safe food and water. Knowledge of the capacities and intentions of adversaries was limited. Violence within and between nation-states and empires was frequent, for a multitude of reasons. Human life was cheap.

How did these sharp scarcities in resources, knowledge and safety affect the international system, especially the causes and course of war? These scarcities interacted, compounding and amplifying each other to make for a very dangerous, violent world. Competing over inadequate resources drove intense geopolitical rivalries as states and empires sought to secure, exploit and defend limited means. A lack of information deepened suspicion, fear and mistrust between political actors. Insecurity and fear for survival increased the likelihood that geopolitical rivalries would become violent.

Great-power war has been driven by multiple factors in the modern era: plunder, dynastic struggles, ideology and revolution, reputation and status, shifts in the military balance of power, vicissitudes in polarity, new military technologies, diversionary strategies, culture and social cohesion, to name a few. There is a deep and often spirited literature that explores these complex issues, and almost as many explanations for past conflicts as there were great-power wars.[12]

In the world of scarcity, where state security was precarious, two variables – territory and population – were central to shaping national interests and power, and compelled the fierce, often violent competition between political actors that drove the scourge of war, conquest and empire that marked modern international relations before the age of plenty. Territory was the most important and contested asset and served as the foundation of state power. Indeed, acquiring and defending land and sea, near and far, while avoiding being conquered, was the foundation of the modern state and the key driver of world politics. As one of the leading scholars of the origins of war explains, 'territory is a general underlying cause of war' and 'of all the possible issues states can fight about, the evidence overwhelmingly indicates that issues involving territory … are the main ones prone to collective violence'. Few 'interstate wars are fought without any territorial issues being involved one way or another'.[13]

What explains the fierce, often violent competition for territory in the age of scarcity? The answer is simple but easily forgotten in the post-industrial age. Sufficient land was essential to provide basic resources for a state's population. Agricultural yields – both crops and livestock – were significantly lower before the era of plenty. They were also highly erratic, with factors such as larger climate shifts, droughts and floods, soil degradation and over-farming often leading to disappointing harvests. If populations grew, more land was needed to feed them. More food meant that surplus populations could be employed in urban areas, generating greater tax revenue for the state, or in the armed forces. Less food meant famine, economic crisis, revolts and vulnerability to invasion. Land also provided the major source of fuel and construction and shipping materials, in the form of timber (and later coal, iron ore and petroleum). Expanding their territory allowed states to develop burgeoning overland and overseas market economies, and equally importantly, afforded defence in depth against adversarial neighbours whose intentions and capabilities were difficult to ascertain.

Gaining more land and control of the sea also allowed a state to support larger populations. In terms of power in the world of scarcity, the size of a state's population pulled in different directions. On the one hand, more people could translate to greater strength: if a state's economy could effectively employ greater numbers of people, its economic production would generate increased wealth, which could be converted into more powerful state and military capabilities. On the other, larger numbers of people could be a burden. Increased populations put greater strains on limited resources: more food, fuel and shelter had to be found somewhere, or these populations could face famine or disease, or be the source of uprisings or war. As the Reverend Thomas Malthus observed at the turn of the nineteenth century, 'population, when unchecked, increases in a geometrical ratio. Subsistence increases only in an arithmetic ratio.'[14]

When increasing numbers of people pressured finite resources needed to live, 'rebalancing' – or increased deaths through famine, disease or war – often took place until the population returned to 'equilibrium'. The world population in 400 CE was not much greater than it had been in 400 BCE and it did not double again until 1100 CE, 15 centuries later. Calculating population in the past is difficult, but because of rebalancing, the number of people in the world may have declined by as much as 10% between 1250 and 1300; 21% between 1340 and 1400;[15] and perhaps by one-third between 1618 and 1690.[16]

Involuntary 'demographic compression' could be a brutal process. Francis Bacon reminded leaders that states should 'ensure that their subjects, unless "mowen downe by wars, does not exceed the stock of the kingdome that should maintain them", as a prolonged imbalance between the production and consumption of food sooner or later produces famine, disruption, and revolt'.[17] This is what happened in the mid-seventeenth century, as, in the words of the historian Geoffrey Parker, the 'dramatic reduction in the food supply around the world … whether through human or natural agency … forced many human communities to take urgent and extreme measures to reduce their food consumption'. By 1680, after a variety of catastrophes, including war, rebellion, famine and disease, severely reduced populations from China and Japan to India and throughout Europe, the world returned to equilibrium.[18] A similar global 'die-off' had taken place in the fourteenth century during the Black Death.

This interactive and explosive relationship between population and land changed dramatically, first in Great Britain around 1750, then in Europe and much of Asia after 1850. Beginning with increased agricultural productivity, followed by industrialisation, better medical practices, sanitation, public health and other factors, death rates decreased while birth rates increased, breaking the pattern of population equilibrium that had long prevailed. The population of Europe, which had been nearly static for centuries, doubled in the eighteenth century and doubled again in the nineteenth.[19] Similar increases took place in East Asia. On the one hand, the growing population was both created by and fed into increased industrialisation and urbanisation, which generated greater wealth and state capacity, which was often used for territorial expansion. On the other, it generated enormous domestic and international instability and dangers. Millions were forced to leave agricultural settings for precarious lives in dangerous, squalid, overcrowded cities, finding erratic employment while unmoored from the traditions and social safety net of the farms and villages they left behind. In England, the proportion of the population living in cities grew from 20% in 1801 to 80% in 1911.[20] In Germany, the proportion of the population living in settlements of over 2,000 people grew from 36% in 1871 to 60% in 1910.[21] Governments often viewed these new populations with suspicion, seeing them as expensive burdens during difficult times, and tinder for revolts, assassinations and uprisings against the regime. Increasing populations also made leaders think about the need and opportunities to seize more territory, near and far. As McNeill pointed out, 'growing populations do not voluntarily leave their neighbours alone and at ease within existing economic, political, and social networks'.[22]

Rapidly increasing populations often generated turbulence, be it war, imperial activity or revolution. Summarising the history of the modern world, McNeill argued that the 'rule of thumb whereby growing populations may be expected to sustain a politics of expansion' was 'borne out by events since 1750'.[23] From the French Revolution, the Napoleonic Wars, British industrialisation, migration and accelerated imperialism to the 'military convulsions of the twentieth century' that

led to total, global war, a key source of international political upheaval was the 'collision between population growth
and limits set by traditional modes of living'.[24] This was
not simply a European phenomenon: the Japanese Empire
justified its expansion by the requirements for territory and
resources driven by population growth.[25]

The typical competition for territory and markets intensified as populations increased. Leaders not only saw their own
subjects needing more land and resources; they witnessed
the populations of rival states and empires increasing, and
feared that their competitors would grow more powerful,
and perhaps dominate the seas and grab scarce land and
markets first. The notion of a fierce, life-or-death competition
for finite resources and 'living space' had become commonplace by the late nineteenth century, and was an explicit
part of official justifications for war in 1914 (especially in
imperial Germany), and, as historian Alison Bashford notes,
this continued after the calamity of the First World War.
'From the beginning, German fascists nurtured ambitions to
expand both population and land, fully incorporating early
geopolitical ideas.'[26] This was not simply a German idea. 'The
Lebensraum (living space) argument that came to characterize
German fascism was not dissimilar to positions commonly
held by US, British, Indian, and Australasian demographers,
economists, or geographers: that overpopulated countries
did have a claim to land, a need for "territorial outlets".'[27]
The idea of the Malthusian 'struggle for room and food'
combined with social Darwinism and the idea of the 'survival
of the fittest' to form the core of geopolitical thinking in
the late nineteenth to mid-twentieth century that shaped
how analysts and policymakers viewed international relations. The historian James Joll argued that it is impossible
to understand the enthusiastic rush to war in Europe during

the summer of 1914 without recognising the pervasive influence of a 'doctrine of a perpetual struggle for survival and of a permanent potential war of all against all' that emerged from a dangerous mix of social Darwinism and popularised if misunderstood Nietzschean thought.[28] Avner Offer notes that the British geopolitical theorist Halford Mackinder and the US naval strategist Alfred T. Mahan were both 'affected by current notions of social Darwinism that regarded nations and especially races as engaged in a constant struggle in which only the "fittest" would survive'. For many, 'international relations (and sometimes domestic social relations as well)' was depicted 'as a desperate struggle'.[29]

War, revolution and imperial conquest were not new in the late nineteenth century and first half of the twentieth century. The intensity, magnitude and reach of this violence, however, was startling. The story of how European powers exploited their vastly increased industrial wealth and new technologies married to powerful military organisations bound by increased national fervour is well known. European imperialism stretched around the globe, subjugating hundreds of millions of people to exploitative and often cruel colonial rule. First European powers, then states in Asia, fought bloody wars of conquest and suppression that killed not only millions of soldiers, but tens of millions of civilians as well. Even the supposedly anti-imperialist US was briefly gripped by the desire for overseas territorial empire, from Puerto Rico to the Philippines, Hawaii and other Pacific holdings. Mass killings of innocents based on racial, ethnic, religious and other sociocultural features became commonplace. Revolution, hyper-nationalism and radical ideologies marked the poisoned international political landscape.

The causes of these cataclysms that rocked world politics are deeply contested and complex. For the purposes of this essay, the key point is how, despite growing wealth and power, states and empires were driven to compete ruthlessly and violently for resources and sources of security that were scarce, or believed to be scarce, in a world lacking information and burdened by mistrust. In retrospect and by certain measures, the period from the late nineteenth century onwards looks like one of impressive economic growth and innovation. Population pressures would soon start to ease. Yet while aspects of plenty were emerging, few recognised the change. The historical legacy of scarcity conditioned people to expect this success to stall and even reverse. Resources had always been limited – there was no historical precedent for the massive increases in wealth continuing unimpeded – and once populations grew beyond the ability of political actors to support them, disaster had always inevitably struck. One way to stave off or limit such catastrophes and to ensure survival was to seize further territory, near and far, be it through market penetration, imperial rule or outright annexation. States and empires that did not organise themselves effectively to compete, to expand and acquire more territory risked being penetrated, exploited and carved up themselves. In the eighteenth century, China and the Ottoman Empire were two of the most powerful, advanced, populous and sprawling empires the world had ever seen, but by the end of the nineteenth century their sovereignty, power and territory had been dramatically reduced, their survival was in doubt and their fates shaped by external powers.

Why does this history matter? Many factors and choices drove the horrific chaos and bloody conflicts that upended world politics between the end of the nineteenth century and the first half of the twentieth century. A key driver was the effort to escape the clutches of scarcity, real or perceived, which drove ever more expensive and lethal imperial projects and great-power wars, and which encouraged a particular form of state-building and society. This period might be thought of as one of neo-scarcity, when new technologies and the socio-economic upheaval brought by mass industrialisation combined with exploding populations, especially in Europe, to make conquest and imperialism, as well as radical ideologies and revolutionary fervour, increasingly prevalent. Asymmetric and historically anomalous military advantages allowed the European and Japanese empires to seize enormous amounts of territory, dominate the seas and control large populations throughout the world. These same technologies made European continental and East Asian rivalries especially dangerous and bloody.

States and empires that could effectively translate new industrial wealth into projectible military power, unify their populations through shared ideologies and identities, and focus their governing efforts on this fierce competition managed to survive and even, for a time, thrive. The relationship between the modern state and war, always intimate, grew closer. Trade brought wealth but was typically understood as a tool in the fierce, zero-sum international competition, rather than as a vehicle for greater interdependence and peace. Cooperation was elusive, international institutions virtually non-existent, and alliances in this dark world were entirely instrumental, temporary, and easily abandoned or reversed.

International politics from the late nineteenth century to the middle of the twentieth century, shaped by scarcity and fears of scarcity, were even more turbulent, violent and often repressive than in the past. Yet as the next section will describe, powerful though unrecognised historical forces were altering the underlying causes of this intensified violence and instability. As a result, today's international system is dramatically different. Unfortunately, our contemporary theories of international relations, and the policy recommendations that emerge from them, are too often shaped by the memories of a world that has largely disappeared.

II. The taming of scarcity and the end of empire

The conclusion of the Second World War ended an especially murderous, chaotic period in world history. Between the late nineteenth and mid-twentieth centuries, wars, revolutions and rebellions, ethnic cleansing and genocide took the lives of tens of millions of people and disrupted the lives of hundreds of millions more. This violence and chaos were different in magnitude, though not in type, from the wars, rebellions and catastrophes, both natural and human-made, that had long marked global politics in the modern era. As in times past, protracted war brought human misery through the second- and third-order effects of conflict, such as famine, disease, extreme poverty and forced migration, fire and flood, massacres, and political repression and tyranny.

This catastrophic turbulence had many sources, but a primary driver was the desire by states and empires to conquer territories near and far in order to overcome often extreme scarcity or the fear of future scarcities in economic resources, information and security. The intense competition between states and empires generated feedback loops of increasing scarcities: lack of information, markets, resources or security led to expansion, sometimes deliberative, other times preventive, to avoid being conquered.

In 1945, as decades of global war and turbulence slowed, one question dominated all others: would the future resemble the past? Many observers assessing the hellscape of destruction, human misery and unresolved tensions in the aftermath of the Second World War might have predicted that the world would indeed remain shaped by intense scarcity and pervasive conquest. There was little reason to think that the underlying dynamics of the international system would change. The social Darwinian world view and Malthusian pressures of increasing populations draining limited quantities of basic resources seemed to get worse, not better: it seemed that populations would continue their geometric increases and that the availability of basic resources would struggle to keep pace. While the German and Japanese empires had been defeated, other European empires worked diligently and violently to recover or retain their colonies, or at least some of them. The threat of power vacuums, revolts and rebellions, extreme ideologies and inter-state war haunted international politics. The global economy was devastated, production and trade had collapsed, and cities, villages and farm assets had been decimated. The sharp ideological and geopolitical divides between the Soviet Union and the US all but guaranteed deepening conflict and perhaps a third world war, this time with the frightening prospect of atomic weapons being used. This pessimistic view informed the emerging academic field of international relations in the US, whose theorists – many of whom were either themselves émigrés or were influenced by émigrés who had fled the horrors of Europe – based their world views on the expectation that Hobbesian anarchy, scarcity and precarity of individual and state survival were permanent features of the international system.

Those observers, however, were wrong. The future did not resemble the past. There was, to be sure, further great violence, as civil wars and conflicts between states continued. In the years since 1945, however, fully mobilised wars of conquest between great powers have largely disappeared, while formal empire has faded. Over time, territorial sovereignty and integrity became a valued norm, followed decades later by human rights. State survival became far less precarious. Unprecedented amounts of wealth, information and security were generated, first in the developed world, then over far larger parts of the planet. Between 1920 and 2020, the average human lifespan doubled.[30] Additionally, most people's quality and diversity of life improved dramatically, violence of all sorts fell, and relative stability, rather than chaos, marked governance. The last three-quarters of a century has been, historically, an age of unparalleled, previously unimaginable plenty.

Why did scarcity and imperial conquest cease to dominate the world, as they had for centuries past? There were many drivers, but five tectonic shifts – revolutions affecting every aspect of individual and political life in the developed world, if not the whole world – upended international politics, taming scarcities and creating, compared to previous periods, an era of plenty. As a result, the international system was utterly transformed, making it unrecognisable from the past.

Revolution 1: voluntary demographic compression

Throughout history, prosperous times, measured by growing wealth and stability, brought increased population, generated by earlier marriage, increased fecundity and lower death rates. Eventually, however, these population increases put pressure on the limited resources available to feed, house and employ people. Before 1750, high mortality and fertility rates meant that populations maintained an almost perfectly balanced birth-to-death ratio.[31] The only consistent demographic trend was that various catastrophes, including war, famine and disease, visited vulnerable populations and increased death rates, returning populations to a sustainable equilibrium.[32]

This age-old law of demographics no longer applies in the era of plenty. Despite extraordinarily good times, measured by wealth, health and safety, people in the developed world have far fewer children than they did in the past. Though people were unaware it was happening at the time, European fertility began to decline in 1890, signalling the start of the 'demographic transition', which has since spread to many other parts of the world.[33] Marriage takes place later if at all, contraception is widespread, equality and education for women have emerged, and many developed nations reproduce at far lower than the replacement rate. Not only did populations in richer countries, after some post-war increases, stabilise; they are in many cases falling. The composition of the population in the developed world is also much older. Americans aged over 65 are projected to compose 9% more of the population in 2040 than in 1990, and Canadians over 65 will make up 25.3% of the population in 2040.[34] 'Like an avalanche, the demographic forces – pushing toward more deaths than births – seem to be expanding and accelerating.'[35] Demographic compression is spreading beyond the developed world, and demographers predict that peak global population will arrive in the 2060s or 2070s at the latest, before beginning a steep decline.

Stable or declining older populations remove one of the key drivers of conquest, empire and great-power war, as states no longer need to seek additional territory or to export soldiers or migrants to reduce population pressures. McNeill noted that 'shrinking populations are not likely to sustain expansion abroad'.[36] Older populations are less violent. Large youth components drive violence in those countries without the economic and social means to absorb them, and make societies more tolerant of high-casualty warfare.[37] But stable and even declining populations, with older citizens, generate other important challenges for wealthier societies. Ageing populations put far greater pressure on social-welfare systems – caring for the elderly is expensive, especially as they leave the workforce – thus these societies need the thinning slice of productive young citizens to be engaged in tax-generating economic enterprises, rather than being a fiscal drain as soldiers fighting expensive wars of conquest and occupation.

Revolution 2: economic transformation

The amount of wealth the world generates – and how it is created – is historically unprecedented in the age of plenty. 'The world's GDP per capita rose 185% between 1950 and 2000, or 2.1% per annum', observe the economist Ronald Findlay and the historian Kevin H. O'Rourke. 'When compared with the centuries of relative stagnation prior to 1800, or indeed with the modest (but at the time unprecedented) growth rates of the British Industrial Revolution, or of the nineteenth century, this performance is quite simply astonishing.'[38] This growth has only accelerated and spread more widely since the turn of the twenty-first century. Global GDP per capita in 1960 was merely US$457; in 2022 it was US$12,647.[39] This wealth has allowed for dramatic improvements in life, and not only in the developed world. Other indices of human development, from life expectancy to education, have dramatically increased.

This economic transformation, part of which had its roots in the nineteenth century and even earlier, had many causes. Four of these, however, are especially relevant to the reduction of imperial conquest and great-power war.

Firstly, an agricultural revolution produced astounding growth in the amount, variety and predictability of food available to the developed world, while driving down its cost. Several changes, from better farming and soil science to improved animal-husbandry practices, and veterinary science and antibiotics, helped increase agricultural productivity, but three factors in particular transformed the global food supply into the historically unprecedented source of abundance it is today: mechanisation, fertilisation and plant breeding. Mechanisation first transformed American farmland, turning the US into the world's breadbasket. American agricultural productivity was astonishing between 1840 and 1910: domestic wheat output increased by 653%, oats by 690% and corn by 695%.[40] In the 100 years that followed, American agricultural production further increased nearly fivefold, despite massive decreases in labour inputs.[41] Europe, already marked by over-farmed land, responded to America's success with technological innovations, the most important of which was to manufacture fertiliser in the early twentieth century through the Haber–Bosch process. This allowed farmers to plant high-demand cereal crops at consistent rates on intensely farmed land, dramatically increasing agricultural output without the need for expanded acreage.[42] Though innovations in mechanical equipment and synthetic fertilisers were essential for producing greater crop yields, however, the most important factor transforming global agricultural output was the development of high-yield seed varieties after the Second World War. Even though the developing world lacked similar developments in agricultural mechanisation, the pairing of novel varieties and nitrogen synthetic fertilisers, in addition to other innovations such as pesticides, would also produce remarkable abundance.

These agricultural innovations combined with improvements in preserving food, such as canning, preservatives and refrigeration, and cheaper transportation. This produced massive increases in the amount and variety of food and equally impressive decreases in the cost of food that could be grown on an acre of land, and allowed the output to be processed, stored and delivered anywhere in the world. In short, far less land was needed to produce far more food. Similar innovations vastly increased livestock production and the availability of meat. In the developed world, the spectre of famine receded, and in time, these benefits spread globally. Remarkable innovations such as lab-grown foods, genetically modified crops and seeds resistant to extreme weather promise to expand this plenty further.

The second cause of the economic transformation was an energy revolution. The availability and efficiency of fuel skyrocketed, while its cost plummeted, as the developed world moved from human and animal labour, then water, to timber, then coal, to petrochemicals, then to greatly increased efficiency with fossil fuels, to today's mix of fossil fuels and renewables. Fuel costs as a percentage of GNP fell dramatically in the developed world between 1945 and today; the price and availability of heating and housing improved; and the cost of manufacturing and transportation plummeted while the range and volume of movement expanded, vastly increasing global trade.

Thirdly, an industrial-productivity revolution led to enormous increases in economic output, driven by extraordinary technological innovations, improved management practices, political stability, and the availability of literate, numerate, healthy workers. A key difference from nineteenth-century industrialisation has been the improved ability of developed societies to absorb and integrate hundreds of millions of rural migrants into the urban and suburban world without the chaos, misery and violence this process often unleashed in previous centuries. New technologies, such as artificial intelligence (AI), promise to continue these productivity advances, assuming their benefits can be balanced with the socio-economic disruptions they may bring.

Fourthly, financial practices were transformed. Widespread improvements and innovations in capital formation and distribution, lending and investing provided entities from large states to individuals with access to flexible, deep and historically cheap sources of capital. These funds could be used for any number of purposes, including investing in transformative technologies that increased productivity, infrastructure that improved lives, consumer goods, or a rainy-day fund that allowed institutions or individuals to ride out unexpected disasters without ruin. The unprecedented fiscal, monetary and financial measures carried out by the developed world during the COVID-19 pandemic have, to the great surprise of most, appeared to fulfil John Maynard Keynes's long-ago prediction that 'anything we can actually do we can afford'.[43]

Revolution 3: information

Throughout most of human history, knowledge about both the natural and the human-made world was scarce to non-existent. The scientific revolution increased humankind's understanding of, and, in time, control over nature. Knowledge of the social and political world – including the inclinations, intentions and capabilities of potential enemies – was slower to come by. When information about the world did exist in the age of scarcity, it was expensive, disseminated slowly and unverifiable, and it competed with, and often lost out to, faith, myth and superstition when decisions were made. It was typically jealously controlled by small numbers in elite institutions.

Several factors vastly increased the level of knowledge, and perhaps as importantly, lowered its cost and universalised its distribution. Mass public education – a rarity before the age of plenty – dramatically broadened and deepened mass literacy and numeracy. Research institutes and the modern research university emerged, expanded and spread globally, and with them, widespread training and research in science, engineering, law and social sciences. Newspapers, radio, television and the internet provided exponential growth in access to unlimited information about the world for almost anyone, increasingly not intermediated by legacy institutions such as religious authorities or the state. The amount and speed of accessing knowledge has exploded while the cost of generating and disseminating it has plummeted. Satellites and sensors provide information about what is happening anywhere and everywhere in the world in real time, including the movements of adversaries. The chance of being conquered by a surprise attack has fallen enormously, although not entirely disappeared.

In the past, information scarcity often generated fear, and fear often contributed to poor decision-making, instability, tyranny and violence. More knowledge and a better understanding of both the natural world and the social and political one often helped ease those fears and allowed for more thoughtful, deliberative decision-making. New technologies and higher levels of education will only deepen and expand this trend.

Revolution 4: governance, domestic and global

The state is often thought of as an entity designed to protect its citizens from both domestic and foreign dangers. Before the middle of the twentieth century, however, few states either fully embraced or were able to consistently deliver on this mission. Governments around the world were often helpless in the face of common depredations like famine, drought, flood, fire, disease, crime and violence, and misery. Political injustice, incompetence and state exploitation often worsened these ills. Even successful wars carried out by the state inflamed these miseries, as well as bringing the horrors of battle, with few benefits, to its citizens.

Governance has been revolutionised in the age of plenty. The science of public administration dramatically improved the ability of local, regional and national governments to provide services including but not limited to sewer, waste and water management; public health and access to medical care; improved roads and transportation; widespread electrification; mass cost-free schooling; building and fire-safety regulations; crowd control; and policing and criminal justice. The massive expansion in the level and effectiveness of citizen services offered by the state has been startling, making countries far safer and healthier than they were in the past. The social welfare of its citizens increasingly became the state's main purpose: guaranteeing education, medical care, safety and steady employment, and supporting those experiencing sickness, misfortune, poverty and old age. One reason that states were able to dramatically shift their resources and focus from war and conquest to social welfare is that state survival was under far less threat. Furthermore, widespread education, access to information and democratisation meant that governments were, unlike in the past, held accountable for whether or not they kept their citizens safe and well. If a government did not perform effectively in this regard, it could be replaced in elections. Even non-democracies are increasingly expected to deliver safety and prosperity to meet their citizens' needs or face consequences.

Improved governance was especially marked in economic policy. The rise of the field of modern economics allowed states and their new institutions to use monetary, fiscal and social-welfare policy to manage and often avoid the 'slumps' that had plagued societies in the past. Alleviating poverty became a key goal, and unemployment insurance, welfare and social security provided a safety net to protect vulnerable citizens. Ruinous bouts of inflation decreased in frequency.

International economic governance also improved, as new institutions like the IMF, established in 1944, and the Bank for International Settlements, established in 1930, supplemented increased communications, coordination and cooperation between governments, central banks and private-sector banks. The result has been remarkable – despite financial crises, recessions, natural disasters and the fluctuations of the business cycle, the world economy has not suffered a 'depression' in almost a century. Over that time, well-understood rules, institutions and practices in the international economy have led to a massive increase in the freer global movement of goods, money and ideas, making formal empire and imperial arrangements increasingly superfluous.

The revolution in governance even affected the anarchic world of international politics. Although it is, to say the least, imperfect, the United Nations helped enshrine territorial sovereignty as a norm and provided institutions to protect its member states. Though far from consistently pursued, human rights and the welfare of people around the world are increasingly understood as a global responsibility. Security arrangements and alliances that spanned the globe were developed, dampening tensions while deterring conflict. Other regional partnerships and groupings have proliferated. In the age of scarcity, alliances between states were temporary, additive, threat-specific and under-institutionalised, whereas today they are often lasting and deep. Expansive missions are supported by often permanent, fully staffed organisations, allowing states to spend less rather than more on military capabilities. Perhaps the most remarkable of these arrangements has been the project of the European Union. Europe, the global cockpit for many of the world's wars of conquest and empire for centuries, is now increasingly integrated, with war between EU members almost unthinkable.

Revolution 5: thermonuclear weapons

The First World War killed around 20m soldiers and civilians.[44] As horrific as that was, the Second World War was even worse, killing 70–85m, or 3% of the world population.[45] Additionally, tens of millions more people were killed by the Spanish flu pandemic of 1918–19, revolutions and wars between the two global conflagrations. New military technologies married to the ability of the modern state to fully mobilise its citizens and deploy its whole society towards total war brought the lethality of conflict to new levels.

Was any political goal worth these costs? As John Mueller has argued, the horrors inflicted by two world wars may have induced a deep aversion to total war around the globe, making conflict far less likely even in the absence of the thermonuclear revolution.[46] New technology, however – first atomic/fission, then hydrogen/fusion bombs – threatened to increase the cost of war many times over. Two atomic bombs, dropped by the US on the Japanese cities of Hiroshima and Nagasaki in 1945, killed perhaps over 200,000 people. Thermonuclear weapons, developed in the early 1950s, have the potential to be as much as 1,000 times more powerful than those bombs. In the decades after the Second World War, the improved ability to deliver these fearsome thermonuclear weapons, first via long-range bombers, then intercontinental missiles launched from land or sea, meant that unimaginable devastation could be inflicted on any part of the globe in less than 30 minutes. At the height of the Cold War, a full-scale nuclear exchange between the Soviet Union and the US would have killed hundreds of millions of people from the blast, thermal radiation, fires and local fallout. More may have died from the likely collapse of the economic, political and social functioning of the societies attacked. Unknown environmental effects may have endangered the whole planet.

The horror of nuclear war dramatically reduced the appeal of invasion and conquest. What state would risk invading a nuclear-armed adversary, knowing that its efforts to conquer territory might earn it a devastating nuclear attack that destroyed its own country? As the US offered security guarantees – or its 'nuclear umbrella' – to allies around the world, even more territory seemed off limits to invasion (and without that umbrella, many more states might have acquired nuclear weapons to provide 'invasion insurance'). Despite deep international tensions and outright hostility between the two leading powers in the system, the Soviet Union and the US, the thermonuclear revolution reduced the odds of full-scale, great-power war, causing the Cold War to become what John Lewis Gaddis called the 'long peace'. And, to an extent that would have likely surprised observers in 1945 or 1960, nuclear weapons have been managed and governed in a way that has limited their spread and forestalled their use in war.

Plenty, not plunder: the changing nature of power

There is little doubt that human life has been transformed during the age of plenty. Overpopulation is no longer a problem in the developed world and people live far longer than ever before. Diverse, predictable and plentiful food is available at historically low cost, and famine is rare. In advanced economies, affordable energy, transportation and housing abound, as do clean water, medical care, education and public safety. Unlimited amounts of information are available to anyone, at almost no cost. Violence on both the personal and the political level has steeply fallen. Governments are expected to produce for their citizens, not vice versa. Great depressions appear to be a thing of the past. People live far longer, are better fed, housed and clothed, are safer and are better governed than at any time in recorded human history. Wealth, information and security, once scarce, are now, historically speaking, relatively plentiful.

How do these profound changes in how humans live and interact affect the international system, and in particular, questions of great-power war and peace? Many causes of war and conflict have not disappeared during the age of plenty and will likely never disappear entirely. However, some of the most important drivers of war in the past – namely plunder and imperial conquest – do not make sense today. Nor are the kinds of total, fully mobilised wars that shaped the first half of the twentieth century optimal or likely.

One of the great drivers of war in history was simple plunder, or the idea that it is productive and economically rational to seize and exploit (or eliminate), through force, the assets, wealth and people of a competing political entity. This is no longer a driver of developed state behaviour; if it were, the US would have taken Canada decades ago. States instead invest resources far more wisely in other, more profitable activities at home, while engaging in global trade and finance to take advantage of the laws of comparative advantage abroad. More complicated than simple plunder and annexation is formal empire, which often operates through a mixture of coercion, exploitation, appeasement and elite entrapment in conquered territories. Imperial occupation no longer makes much sense, as the benefits of conquest have fallen precipitously, while the costs of controlling and ruling an empire have risen dramatically.

In the past, it made sense for states to acquire territory, near or far, in order to secure scarce resources such as food, energy and markets, or employment for excess population – either as imperial migrants or soldiers – and to provide defence in depth. The economic and demographic revolutions have removed these drivers. More food can be produced on less land, and populations have stabilised in the developed world. As a result, territory is a far less important component of well-being and state power than it once was. Wealth and power are far more likely to be generated by better ideas and innovations than by acquiring more land.

Even if a state did desire more land, the costs of invasion, conquest and occupation are now prohibitive, even without considering the potential danger of nuclear escalation. The US, the most militarily and economically powerful state in the world, failed in its efforts to occupy two states, Iraq and Afghanistan, which were no military match, despite spending trillions of dollars and deploying the most sophisticated military tools in the world. Russia, with far more 'power' than Ukraine as measured by traditional metrics, has failed in its effort to subdue its smaller, far less powerful neighbour.

A less recognised but equally important factor also reduces the appeal of conquest. One of the outcomes of the dramatic lengthening and improvement of life, combined with voluntary demographic compression, has been an increased focus on the individual and their freedom. With the potential for a long life and an array of possibilities in front of them, people in the developed world live according to their individual preferences, rather than to produce as many children as possible or to serve as vassals to a lord, religion or empire. It is no coincidence that this process of generating abundance has led to a rights revolution. As the age of plenty has unfolded, a norm of tolerance and individuality has emerged and strengthened. In much of the developed world, discriminating on the basis of race, ethnicity, religion, gender or sexual orientation is discouraged if not banned – attitudes that were largely unthinkable before quite recently. A world of curated individuality may make it more difficult to mobilise a population to risk their lives and livelihoods on behalf of a goal like conquest or empire; it is certainly more difficult to occupy and co-opt a population with a strong belief in the sanctity of its personal freedoms.

Not only have ideas and innovation replaced land as a source of power, but attraction is often a more powerful tool than coercion for getting one's way in the age of plenty. In the same period during which the US failed to transform the greater Middle East through the use of force, it has increased its dominance of the global sociocultural and economic sphere through cutting-edge companies including Airbnb, Amazon, Apple, Facebook/Meta, Google, Microsoft, Tinder and Uber, financed in creative ways by (largely American) banks, hedge funds, investment banks and venture-capital firms. It has also overseen a technological revolution in fossil-fuel recovery (fracking and liquefied natural gas) that transformed it from a massive energy importer to an exporter. These and other innovations over the past two decades have, arguably, had a far greater effect on advancing its interests and values than any counter-insurgency or nation-building campaign.

At times, the US government can embrace this kind of innovation and forward-thinking grand strategy. At the same time as the administration of George W. Bush launched its disastrous war in Iraq, it also unveiled the President's Emergency Plan for AIDS Relief (PEPFAR) to help reduce the suffering caused by AIDS in Africa – an effort that is estimated to have saved 25m lives.[47] It is clear which policy did far more to advance America's interest and reputation, while making the world a better place.

Indeed, technological prowess in telecommunications, energy and health, financial muscle, political openness and responsiveness, generosity and sociocultural attraction – 'soft power' – enhance or are often better indicators of global rank than measures from the past world like quantities of tanks or battleships, ethno-national unity, or coal, wheat and steel production. Adding territory, acquiring colonies or occupying foreign lands is rarely attractive in today's world. Demographic growth is flat and even declining in many advanced economies; ageing, shrinking populations rarely drive state conquest. While circumstances could change, few of the leading powers need be consumed by fears that they will be conquered or cannot feed their population or access scarce resources or markets. Collective identities are increasingly fractured and hard to maintain, and history has significantly shrunk the menu of broadly appealing, convincing, parsimonious ideologies to unify a population towards a common cause. The digital revolution provides more literate populations with access to extraordinary amounts of information, weakening the role of various institutional intermediaries, including the bureaucratic state, in shaping culture and identity preferences.

The taming of scarcity has profoundly transformed how human beings live and largely removed the powerful incentives that once drove imperial conquest and great-power war. Do these profound transformations in the nature of power and the structure and incentives shaping the international system mean that the world can look forward to a stable, safe and secure future? Not necessarily.

III. The problems of plenty

The taming of economic, informational and security scarcity was the result of at least five world-altering historical revolutions over the past century. These have generated largely beneficial developments, massively improving the length and quality of life for billions of people while fostering endless new opportunities. It is unsurprising that in the age of plenty the occurrence and lethality of conflict fell sharply in the developed world, and the modern state shifted its focus from war to the social welfare of its citizens.[48] There are, no doubt, countless exceptions, and no guarantee that these circumstances will continue. It would make sense to sustain and build upon this success in taming scarcity, and in particular, to spread the benefits of this abundance to areas and societies that do not currently enjoy them.

That said, the tectonic forces, processes, practices and institutions that succeeded in taming scarcity generated, quite unexpectedly and rapidly, a new set of potentially catastrophic planetary challenges: the problems of plenty. Far more than the problems of scarcity, these challenges are numerous, complex, unpredictable and polarising, interact with each other in powerful but mysterious ways, and are often difficult to grasp. Writ large, however, the problems of plenty fall into five broad categories, whereby the danger has become *too much*, not too little: too much production, transmission, communication and information, identity and choice, and expectation. As a result, the state of the international system looks more like the treasure island, generating grave threats that the world is currently ill-prepared to confront.

Production

Taming economic scarcity has generated unimaginable wealth. The processes involved in producing overwhelming amounts of food, fuel, factories, buildings, means of transport and consumer goods has, however, unleashed a litany of problems of plenty. Astoundingly, human-made mass now exceeds all biomass on earth. On average, for each person on the globe, 'anthropogenic mass equal to more than his or her bodyweight is produced every week'.[49] Some think that a mass species extinction event is approaching, which scientists believe would be the sixth such disaster in earth's history.[50] As

Jonathan S. Blake and Nils Gilman list, the threats to human welfare, life and the planet itself generated by production abundance include

> climate change, pandemic diseases, stratospheric ozone depletion, atmospheric aerosol loading, space junk, growing antibiotic resistance, biodiversity loss, anthropogenic genetic disruptions, declining soil health, upended nitrogen and phosphorus cycles, freshwater depletion, ocean acidification, oceanic plastics – and maybe even emerging technologies with terraforming potential, like bioengineering and artificial intelligence.[51]

These issues often interact with, compound and amplify each other. Any one of them could generate grave threats, but collectively, they present an unimaginably difficult and worrying global challenge.

Three especially sharp challenges arise from production plenty. The most alarming is the carbon released into the atmosphere, which is creating a climate crisis that could bring about civilisational, if not planetary, extinction. Carbon-dioxide levels in the atmosphere are higher than at any point in human history and have risen more than 50% in the last two centuries.[52] Furthermore, 'atmospheric levels of methane, an even more potent greenhouse gas, are now about 2.5 times their preindustrial levels and steadily rising'.[53] As Blake and Gilman suggest, 'massive, fossil fuel-based industrialization is forcing profound changes to the biochemistry of the planet'.[54] The rise in the earth's temperature has already generated volatile weather patterns and terrifying effects including regular extreme heatwaves, record high temperatures, melting ice caps, rising sea levels and temperatures, floods, desertification and increased possibilities for novel viruses. The summer of 2023 was the hottest ever recorded, which UN Secretary-General António Guterres labelled 'the great boiling', warning that 'the climate breakdown has begun'.[55] An island in the Gulf recorded a heat index of 73.9°C, while the surface temperature of the water approached 37.8°C.[56] Temperatures are expected to continue to rise – even in the highly unlikely event that global, coordinated policies were to dramatically reduce carbon emissions immediately – with unknown but potentially catastrophic consequences. According to the UN Intergovernmental Panel on Climate Change, 'rising seas, melting ice caps and other effects of a warming climate may be irreversible for centuries and are unequivocally driven by greenhouse-gas emissions from human activity'.[57] A recent study argued that 1bn people may be killed by climate change by 2100 if the earth's temperature rises by 2°C or more.[58] As Ville Lähde suggests, 'we are in effect living on a different planet than all the previous human generations – and people around the world are increasingly inhabiting very different planets from each other. Some of them may become uninhabitable pretty soon.' The Cascade Institute describes 'a cascading, runaway failure of Earth's natural and social systems that irreversibly and catastrophically degrades humanity's prospects'.[59] Kate Mackenzie and Tim Sahay warn that the world faces 'planetary instability and disruption of everyday life as burning carbon loads the climate dice so that it throws six after six'.[60] These problems of production plenty are inherently complex, interactive and unpredictable, making policy responses orders of magnitude more challenging.

Consider something as mundane but consequential as making and using concrete, a processed material that revolutionised how people live, and a core tool in taming scarcity.

Few materials better reflect the transformed world. 'Most of humanity now lives in cities made possible by concrete.' Most buildings, bridges, roads, pavements, airports, subways, pipes, sewers, dams and power plants are made solely or largely of concrete. Yet, as Joe Zadeh points out, 'concrete has been like a nuclear bomb in man's conquest of nature'. Producing concrete has forced the redirection of rivers, levelled mountains, contributed to flooding and biodiversity loss, and generated destructive carbon output while using almost 2% of the world's water.[61] Ironically, however, given that it is fireproof, waterproof and resistant to strong winds and rising seas, 'as the climate crisis accelerates and extreme weather events become more common, concrete will be more important than ever'.[62] To add insult to injury, increased carbon in the atmosphere accelerates the deterioration of all this concrete, a material that rarely maintains its structural integrity for more than a century.

The second major issue arising from production plenty is the creation of new, powerful and often complex technologies that tame scarcity and bring great benefits to people, but potentially generate profound and often uncertain dangers. The worry over generative AI models leading to catastrophic dangers – eliminating human control over decision-making, destabilising nuclear deterrents, creating lethal viruses and so forth – is well documented.[63] Other technologies, however, present equally concerning issues. Consider two of many: biogenetics and bioengineering, and additive manufacturing. Bioengineering offers the possibility of treating and even curing previously deadly diseases, including many forms of cancer. Behind that opportunity, however, lurk great dangers. As a recent report cautioned, 'over the coming decades it may become possible for someone to create a pathogen that has been engineered to be substantially more contagious than natural pathogens, more deadly, and/or more difficult to address with standard countermeasures'. But at the same time, 'states or malicious actors with access to these pathogens could use them as offensive weapons'.[64] While the transformative technologies generated by gene-editing techniques such as CRISPR hold the potential to mitigate or cure diseases, gene-editing expert Fyodor Urnov posits that contemporary knowledge and technology would allow heritable editing to be used to create soldiers who need less sleep, have super-physical powers and feel less pain.[65] Additive manufacturing presents a similar dilemma. Productivity may be massively increased, but at the cost of well-paid manufacturing jobs. Lethal, catastrophic weapons could be developed by terrorist groups or even an individual with bad intentions. As a recent RAND study explained, 'the increasing access to and capabilities of AM have the potential to dramatically disrupt the prevailing state system and international order', comparing it with 'the jarring effects of the Industrial Revolution' which 'drove military industrialization, transforming warfare at a catastrophic cost to humanity while simultaneously bringing about incalculable benefits'. Additive manufacturing 'will not only exacerbate many of today's most pressing socioeconomic challenges but also unleash new kinds of security threats'.[66]

These are just two examples of many possible emerging technologies that offer both unimaginable promise and terrifying dangers. Related to these dangers is the issue of who should make the cost–benefit trade-offs between the promise and terror of these new capabilities. Unlike in the past, these new technologies are often driven by the private sector, motivated by profit, as opposed to by the state, driven by common welfare and considerations of national interest. Private-sector incentives are often weakly aligned with the larger public interest and political considerations, and corporations often possess a poor understanding of how technology intersects with larger policy, national-security and international-security considerations.

The third challenge generated by production plenty is inequality, both within and between societies. Increasing global wealth by leaps and bounds obviously affords the resources to tame scarcity by providing previously unimaginable levels and types of goods and services to more and more people. But this production plenty also generates distributional conflicts, as increasing affluence is most often allocated in ways that highlight the relative differences in wealth and status within and between states. Worse, the problems of plenty are largely generated by the richer, more secure countries, who often possess greater resilience and better means to adapt, while unjustly falling hardest on those states and populations who remain closer to scarcity and have not enjoyed the benefits of plenty. Disputes over relative gains – in terms of economics, information and security – can create tensions as easily as clashes over absolute differences. As a recent Brookings Institution report argues, rising inequality stokes global discontent and is

> a major driver of the increased political polarization and populist nationalism that are so evident today. An increasingly unequal society can weaken trust in public institutions and undermine democratic governance. Mounting global disparities can imperil geopolitical stability.[67]

Transmission
A key feature of the age of plenty is the extraordinary ability to move massive quantities of ideas, money, goods and especially

people around the world quickly, irrespective of borders and territory. But this revolution in transmission does not simply enable good citizens and products to move around the world: unwanted agents – from pathogens to terrorists to bad ideas – can also move far more quickly and effortlessly, often with devastating consequences. Indeed, this revolution helped accelerate a globalisation that, while it created wealth and expanded markets, also exacerbated and reshaped an older threat from the world of scarcity: pandemics. As Blake and Gilman highlight, our ability to understand the nature of viral infections has increased exponentially, while our ability to

> control the spread of a pandemic disease has hardly improved at all. At the same time, the globalization of our economic system has only accelerated the rate at which viruses can proliferate. Whereas the Black Death took eight years to march from Kyrgyzstan to Crimea in the 1330s and 1340s and the 1918 influenza took three months to move from Kansas to Europe, SARS-CoV-2 spread from Wuhan to Europe and North America within three weeks, causing public health system meltdowns and thousands of deaths in Lombardy and New York.[68]

Ideas, people, goods, information, money and pathogens do not simply move quickly: they move in complex and explosive ways we do not fully understand or control. This ignorance extends to the 'highly interdependent systems that we do not understand and cannot control well' and that 'are vulnerable to failure at all scales, posing serious threats to society, even when external shocks are absent'. This complexity is only increasing, generating the danger that our 'man-made systems can become unstable, creating uncontrollable situations even when decision-makers are well-skilled, have all data and technology at their disposal, and do their best'.[69]

Information and communication

Before the age of plenty, information was scarce, expensive, centralised in legacy institutions like the state and religious authorities, and disseminated slowly. The digital-telecommunications revolution transformed this situation. All the world's information is now available to many if not most people in the developed world, unfiltered through state or church, almost free of cost, and spread instantaneously. This has generated innumerable benefits to humankind. It has also generated unexpected costs.

The world is flooded with data, which can be challenging to convert to information, to say nothing of knowledge or wisdom. Individuals and even institutions lack the capability to filter, order, collate and make sense of gigantic amounts of data, which leads them to be easily overwhelmed, confused or misled. Determining what data is 'authentic' or relevant in real time, and making sense of it, becomes almost impossible, and polarisation and disinformation often result. As Henry Kissinger argued, 'the digital world's emphasis on speed inhibits reflection; its incentive empowers the radical over the thoughtful; its values are shaped by subgroup consensus, not by introspection. For all its achievements, it runs the risk of turning on itself as its impositions overwhelm its conveniences.'[70]

The development of AI has made this issue significantly more challenging. AI will likely generate many extraordinarily positive benefits to humankind in the years to come. Unregulated, however, experts greatly fear its darker side. As Ian Bremmer and Mustafa Suleyman contend, 'AI could be used to generate and spread toxic misinformation, eroding social trust and democracy; to surveil, manipulate, and subdue citizens, undermining individual and collective freedom; or to create powerful digital or physical weapons that threaten human lives'. It could also eliminate millions of jobs, worsen inequality or 'spark unintended and uncontrollable military escalations that lead to war'.[71]

Few predicted that the digital-telecommunications revolution, which made all information easily accessible to anyone at negligible cost, would have such unsettling consequences. AI is likely to dramatically accelerate these disruptions.

Identity and choice

Throughout much of human history, most people in most places had few choices about how and where they lived their lives, which were often more precarious, poorer and of far shorter duration than they are now. And unless they were involved in a disruptive migration, they probably died near their birthplace; worshipped within the same community and religion as their parents and grandparents; embraced local political and sociocultural traditions; married a partner with a similar background; and had few choices as to a career or vocation. Alternative lifestyles, orientations, preferences or resistance to community standards were rarely tolerated and often fiercely punished.

The age of plenty transformed these circumstances for many, vastly increasing available options and human freedom. An individual could move within or outside their country and exploit numerous educational opportunities to pursue a novel career or hobby. These new options could provide an escape from the tight and often stifling bounds of local community and enable an individual to freely craft an identity around religion, sexual orientation and partnership, sociocultural practices and political commitments. The age of plenty fostered a rights revolution and liberated people from the often-suffocating traditions of their ancestors. This array of choices would have been simply unimaginable in the era of scarcity, reflecting historically unprecedented individual autonomy and independence.

But this otherwise extraordinary development of increasing human freedom came at a cost. While tight communities and traditions can be stifling, they often offer deep connection, a sense of common purpose and a feeling of belonging. Instead of being rooted in a particular place, people in the age of plenty often feel they belong everywhere and nowhere all at once. In this new world, the external infrastructure of sociocultural, economic and even political life is increasingly obscured; the processes that make our lives possible are hidden from sensory view, generating the false sense that empowered individuals are solely the masters of their fates. The visceral sense of 'how things get done' that emerges in tightly bound, traditional societies – where people see and appreciate how vital goods like food and clothing are produced, security procured and information obtained – is lost, potentially making people selfish, incurious and narcissistic. As Joshua Rovner characterises this mindset, 'if Amazon can bring everything to my doorstep in hours or days, then Uncle Sam should too'.[72]

Venerating individualism and encouraging self-crafted identities can weaken the bonds of larger collective enterprises, leaving people isolated, lonely, vulnerable and, at times, dangerously alienated. Arguably, in the age of plenty it is more difficult to convince people to sacrifice individual preferences and personal indulgences on behalf of a larger, shared local, national or planetary mission, or to think along the kind of multigenerational timelines more traditional communities encourage and the problems of plenty demand. Meeting the challenges of plenty will involve the kind of individual sacrifice and collective efforts, made over longer time spans, that were far easier to either compel or obtain in the age of scarcity.

Expectations and governance

The governance revolution in the age of plenty brought enormous benefits, increasing health, safety and well-being around the world. Additionally, markets in goods and capital have delivered a great abundance and variety of consumer goods, technology and innovation to billions of people. As a result, life has vastly improved, at least from a material perspective, for most people. Cities are less likely to burn down or flood; crime is far lower and often solved; clean water, electricity, heating and air conditioning, functioning sanitation, safe food and medicine are widely available; and most people are educated at least until the end of secondary school. These are just a few of the many effective, transformative services offered by governments that were rare in the age of scarcity but are commonplace in developed countries in the era of plenty. People have come to expect high-level results from the state, with their needs met and their security from danger and uncertainty assured. Citizens demand to be protected by their governments from economic slumps and crises, terrorism and invasion – expectations that would have been seen as utopian a century ago. They insist that markets and the state deliver them better and longer lives while continuing to provide unending improvements. As a result, political responsiveness is demanded, and failure punished, either at the ballot box, or through protests or public opinion. And, until recently, states in the developed world have by and large succeeded in meeting these growing expectations.

But what happens when governing institutions and markets do not deliver the services or solutions citizens have come to expect, do not protect people from a great problem or challenge, or even make these problems worse? Unlike people living in the age of scarcity, citizens are used to the state, private markets and the non-profit sector working effectively to cure their ills. Unfortunately, many contemporary institutions and practices, most of which were constructed to deal with issues of scarcity, fare quite poorly when dealing with the newer problems of plenty. They appear unable to lower the summer temperatures in Phoenix; help citizens identify deepfake online messages and disinformation; prevent massive flooding in South Asia; or slow desertification around the globe. Focusing on the climate crisis, the political economist Mark Blyth calls it 'a giant non-linear outcome generator with wicked convexities. In plain English, there is no mean, there is no average, there is no return to normal. It's one-way traffic into the unknown.'[73] Indeed, these institutions appeared especially inept in the face of the most devastating international crisis since the Second World War: the global COVID-19 pandemic, which killed as many as 25m people worldwide between 2020 and 2024.[74] The policies implemented by local, national and international institutions to deal with the pandemic were often erratic, uncoordinated, inconsistent and ineffective.

The combination of citizens' heightened expectations of their state, generated by the unparalleled success at taming scarcity, with the failure of governing institutions to solve or mitigate the problems of plenty has helped drive an increasing loss of faith in governance and markets. Legacy institutions once admired for their success in taming scarcity have lost respect and admiration, and are even sometimes seen as illegitimate. Populist crusaders, often with an authoritarian bent, campaigning against elites, or the 'deep state', have achieved local and national electoral success around the world. Indeed, sometimes super-empowered individuals – such as Elon Musk – acting outside the confines of the state and exploiting new technologies appear to possess more power than the government. This crisis of governing (and market) illegitimacy will deepen as institutions ill-suited to meet the problems of plenty continue to fail in the face of issues like climate change, inequality, public-health crises, migration and disinformation.

IV. Unspoken assumptions, time lags and historical anamnesis

The taming of scarcity and the emerging, potentially existential problems of plenty generate important questions about world politics and grand strategy. In an era of plenty where empire and conquest make little sense, how should we understand the current turmoil in world politics, marked by atrocities in the Middle East, Russia's brutal invasion of Ukraine, and especially the deepening tensions between the world's two most powerful states, China and the US? Relatedly, why are the leading powers seemingly focused on issues that resonated in the world of scarcity, particularly great-power rivalry and war, while offering inadequate responses to the pressing issues generated by a world of plenty? And do experts and leaders currently possess the conceptual, policy and institutional frameworks and capabilities needed to deal with these issues?

Unlike in the age of scarcity, in a world of plenty war is often a poor instrument to achieve national ends. Consider America's decade-plus efforts in Afghanistan and Iraq. The US deployed overwhelming force and cutting-edge technology to achieve military dominance with a relatively light footprint and low casualties. It faced little opposition, possessed a sophisticated policymaker apparatus and was inspired by arguably 'good' motives. Yet despite 'winning' on the battlefield, it ultimately failed in its efforts to occupy and transform either country. Few would argue that America's interests were advanced by either the war in Afghanistan or Iraq, or, from a narrowly power-political perspective, that the wars would have been worth the great human and material cost even if these nation-building occupations had succeeded.

Russia's 2022 invasion of Ukraine is another example of a strategic decision based on outdated assumptions about conquest. From a narrow national-interest perspective, a desire to control the Donbas made some sense in 1900, when its abundant coal, wheat, defence in depth and pliant population added to Russia's power in a world shaped by scarcity and where empire and conquest were the norm. Today, in an age when food and fuel are historically cheap and abundant, land less valuable, conquered territories much more difficult to subdue, alternative grand strategies far more promising, and the world both aghast by and willing to punish Russia for its violations of the norms of sovereignty and human rights, even a successful conquest of Ukraine was unlikely to make Russia much more powerful in the long run. There are obviously many important differences between America's wars in the greater Middle East and Russia's invasion of Ukraine. Both, however, reflect poor grand-strategic decisions based on profound misreadings of the nature of power and the incentives of the contemporary international system, revealing a misunderstanding of the increased difficulty of using force to conquer territories or subdue uncooperative populations in the age of plenty.

A similar puzzle marks the deepening hostility and military competition between China and the US, which is driven in large part by the former's irredentist claims over Taiwan. Most commentators agree that if this rivalry produced a full-scale war between the two most powerful states in the system, it would be, regardless of the outcome, a disaster for both countries and for the world. If China somehow succeeded in conquering Taiwan, it would acquire a disgruntled population at huge military and economic cost, while likely guaranteeing deep global opprobrium, the severing of economic ties, massive military balancing by almost all its neighbours, and Japan and South Korea (at a minimum) joining India and Russia as nuclear-weapons states in their neighbourhood. China would be forced to devote even greater resources to its internal and external security at a time when it possesses few international friends and faces enormous challenges, including a slowing economy, an ageing and shrinking population, deep inequality and growing environmental problems. If China *failed* in its invasion, perhaps thwarted by the US, it might very well escalate, even using nuclear weapons, and continue to try to take Taiwan (and punish those that tried to prevent it from doing so) until it succeeded. Wars, once started, have their own logic, driving far deeper commitments from adversaries than they initially hoped for or anticipated: they are harder to get out of than to start. Unlike in the past, efforts at conquest like this are not only unnecessary for the countries in question to survive and thrive; such wars are more likely to sap the power of the participants. Yet in China, Taiwan and the US, an increasing number of people consider such a conflict likely, if not inevitable.

What about the concern that China's ambitions go far beyond Taiwan, and that it seeks the kind of global domination of past expansive empires? The changing circumstances wrought by the age of plenty make the return of an imperial, ever-expanding Eurasian empire similar to Nazi Germany,

Imperial Japan or Stalin's Soviet Union very unlikely. Unlike states and empires during the age of scarcity, China has no reason to fear being conquered, nor, even if it wanted to, could it easily invade, occupy and take over neighbours like India, Japan and Southeast Asia, especially if a future successful conquest of Taiwan generated widespread military balancing and nuclear proliferation in the region. In the age of plenty, China would soon discover that the cost–benefit ratio of empire and invasion has been completely inverted over the past century. Even if the Chinese Communist Party (CCP) wished to pursue imperial conquest, it is hard to imagine how it could succeed and, if it tried, it would risk its own defeat and collapse.[75]

Why, in an age of plenty, do war and conflict persist, when it is clear that plunder, conquest and formal empire rarely pay? These have been, historically, only one cause of war. Wars can start for many reasons and have been driven by non-material factors such as honour, reputation, regime insecurity and succession struggles, and ideology, to name a few. States can desire territory for reasons other than economic gain. Irredentism is a persistent source of conflict, emerging from unresolved territorial disputes unrelated to scarcity. The tensions in the Middle East, between the Koreas, and between India and Pakistan over Kashmir, and China's desire to incorporate Taiwan, to highlight crucial examples, are, in large measure, motivated by unsettled and often bitter disputes over historical legacy, geography and borders. In other words, states want to recover territories they believe are theirs, even at great cost, and even if the material benefit is uncertain and they are not motivated by scarcity. Irredentism, though it appears similar, is not the same as imperialism. Many wars have had limited aims, falling far short of conquest, empire or territorial revision. Conflict can also arise through misperception, where two or more states misjudge the intentions of the other or, as discussed below, misunderstand the actual state of the international system.

These explanations only go so far in illuminating both the recent past and the current disposition of the major players in the international system. Contemporary great powers often behave as if the world *has not* dramatically changed and is still dominated by geopolitical competition and the threats of widescale conquest and empire. Why do the leading powers in the world (if not most other developed states), both authoritarian and democratic, still appear to analyse and operate in a way more relevant to previous periods of scarcity, as opposed to the current era of plenty?

Despite increased tensions in the international system, states *do not* always behave precisely like they did in the past. Russia's horrific invasion of Ukraine is the exception that proves the rule: such blatant aggression and conquest have been, compared to past historical periods, uncommon among great powers in recent decades, and when they have been attempted, they have rarely succeeded or increased the long-term power prospects of the invader. This aberrant, unexpected occurrence explains part of the widespread focus on Russia's misdeeds, the justified outrage and impressive collective effort to aid Ukraine in its struggle.

And despite the increase in global tensions, military expenditure – either as a percentage of total global GDP or of government expenditure – is stunningly low compared to the past: military spending in 1961 accounted for 6.4% of the world's GDP, whereas 60 years later this figure was only 2.2%. Almost 40% of that current total is spent by one country, the US; adding China's expenditure takes the figure above 50%. In the age of scarcity, most great-power budgets were largely devoted to military outlays; in England, the mean total military spending between the late seventeenth and early nineteenth centuries was almost 75% of government expenditure. As the historian Paul Kennedy pointed out, in the past, 'even in peacetime, the upkeep of the armed services consumed 40 or 50 percent of a country's expenditures; in wartime, it could rise to 80 or even 90 percent of the far larger whole'.[76] The US, despite having a defence budget larger than the next ten countries combined, only devotes 12% of its *federal* expenditure to the armed forces.[77] Russia, which has massively increased its military budget in a desperate struggle to win the war in Ukraine, will still only spend 6% of its GDP on defence in 2024, far less than the 12–17% the Soviet Union spent in an average year during the Cold War.[78] Other developed powers, including former empires such as Britain, France, Germany and Japan, have demonstrated no interest in conquest and, despite recent increases, do not spend much of their impressive national wealth on their armed forces. On certain continents – the Americas, for example – the threat of conquest is virtually non-existent and military spending, outside the US, minimal.

Despite this fall in military spending and the decreasing threat of invasion and conquest, some leading powers behave in ways that may have made sense in the past but are misplaced to confront the realities of the era of plenty. Why? One explanation is that the grand strategies of leading powers are often burdened by unspoken assumptions, historical time lags and historical anamnesis. In other words, it often takes some time – sometimes decades – for people, institutions and states to understand when their environment and circumstances have changed and to update their assumptions, conceptual lenses and policy practices accordingly. In the last century, states, leaders and populations have been slow to recognise that the demographic, agricultural and economic assumptions that shaped their earlier world views and policies had been over-turned. In many cases – such as the lingering fears of imperial conquest and geopolitical domination – these assumptions have still not been fully interrogated and updated. Millennia of conquest, empire and violent revolutions – and governing institutions built to deal with those crises – have left deep scars.

The historian James Joll explained the concept of unspoken assumptions in a brilliant 1968 lecture in which he tried to make sense of how the great powers of Europe plunged into the disastrous and senseless First World War, when a better understanding of international relations would have clearly led them to conclude that the war could and should have been avoided. 'When political leaders are faced with the necessity of taking decisions the outcome of which they cannot foresee, in crises which they do not wholly understand', Joll argued that they often rely on their 'instinctive reactions, traditions and modes of behaviour'.[79] Today's leaders may share the characteristics of their tragic predecessors on the eve of the First World War. Faced with a rapidly changing world and global phenomena they do not understand, they fall back on their long-held, unspoken and often unexamined beliefs about how the world should work, as opposed to trying to better understand how the world does work. Leading powers and their leaders and institutions understand how to confront and tame scarcity, as well as how to play the great-power political game that dominated the past, whereas the problems of plenty, and the solutions required, are unfamiliar and vexing.

Ironically, unspoken assumptions and historical time lags compound another feature of individual and collective human understanding: 'historical anamnesis', or the inability to properly recognise and accept that circumstances are improving. It is incontestable that by almost every measure of human well-being – lifespan, literacy, personal safety and so forth – life is much better for far more people than ever before. The chance that an individual living in the developed world will be affected by the collective ills that plagued the past – fire, flood, famine, deadly illness and especially war – is also tiny compared to previous periods. Applying almost any material metric to individual well-being (such as lifespan, literacy or personal safety), social and political health, or international political stability and security would reveal that the world in 2024 is more safe, stable and prosperous than the world of 1974, which was much better than the world of 1924, which was much more advanced than the world of 1874, which possessed greater wealth and security than that of 1824. As a recent dire diagnosis of the promise and threats of AI pointed out, 'we doubt many readers would like to exchange lives with those born before past industrial revolutions, and the same will almost certainly be the case going forward'.[80] But our politics and institutions do not update their assumptions and world views easily, and instead project often far darker, more pessimistic views of the situation and future than is warranted, failing to recognise that many of the problems of scarcity that drive fears of conquest or the aforementioned collective ills have been impressively tamed.

Past performance is no guarantee of the future; history does not move in a singular, upward direction, and people's circumstances depend to a great extent on their backgrounds and where they live. More importantly, as discussed, the developed world's success in taming scarcity has generated potentially catastrophic planetary challenges, even as personal, collective and institutional responses to these challenges are woefully inadequate. That said, ignoring or misunderstanding positive developments, such as the improved wealth and security that have come during the age of plenty, can be just as foolish as ignoring or underestimating dangers and threats.

In many ways, it is unclear why states do not update their assumptions and continue to pursue suboptimal policies. It is a reminder that contrary to what economic and international-relations theories often suggest, neither people nor states are pure utility maximisers, and great powers routinely choose terrible grand strategies, as Washington's policies in the greater Middle East during the first two decades of the twenty-first century demonstrated. China was the great beneficiary of America's earlier poor choices, but instead of continuing to capitalise on these mistakes, for the past decade it has pursued a grand strategy that has alienated many of its neighbours, aroused the anger of the US, and worried many countries that had once been, if not allies, friendly and admiring of its success. One can construct a plausible counterfactual whereby China, pursuing a smarter grand strategy over the past two decades, would be far closer to achieving its goals surrounding Taiwan, its region and the larger world, at far lower cost, if it had enacted policies that recognised the realities of plenty and were based on attraction rather than coercion. This highlights an often forgotten fact in debates about international relations: tectonic revolutionary forces that ended scarcity and created the world of plenty often emerged *despite* poor state choices.

None of this is a call for the developed world to eliminate military capabilities as a grand-strategic instrument: the international system is obviously full of dangers, and military tools are indispensable. Preventing and punishing aggression and conquest may be an important variable in maintaining and increasing the benefits of a world of plenty and keeping scarcity at bay. States also reasonably desire insurance against the dangers of an unknown future: there is no guarantee that the age of plenty is as benign as suggested, that it will continue, or even if it does, that it would completely subsume powerful historical forces such as nationalism and great-power rivalry that have shaped world politics for centuries.

Overcoming false beliefs about scarcity, however, is of fundamental importance for two reasons. Firstly, if national policies are not updated and if historical anamnesis continues, the world risks a devastating (and, in terms of securing their national interests, pointless) great-power war between China and the US. Secondly, false beliefs about scarcity blind analysts, leaders and policymakers to the novel, more pressing and potentially catastrophic threats to the world – the problems of plenty.

What makes this all the more pressing is that current institutional and governance architecture is inadequate to deal with the daunting and largely unprecedented novel challenges brought about by plenty. It is no wonder, faced with these new, often overwhelming and seemingly intractable challenges, that politics and institutions continue to focus on more familiar issues from the past. Unfortunately, the solutions to the problems of plenty are unlikely to be found in current norms, practices and institutions. The modern nation-state, and much international institutional architecture, was largely designed and constructed to solve the problems of scarcity in a world where the fear of conquest and total war were ever present. Much of this organisational scaffolding is outdated or poorly suited to the problems of plenty. Whereas the problems of scarcity demanded mass mobilisation and unity of purpose, the problems of plenty require nimbleness, innovation, diversity, transparency, adaptability and accountability to maintain governmental and institutional legitimacy.

In a world of nuclear deterrence, integration and inter-dependence, flattening demographics, and abundant food and resources, where the costs of occupation are high and conquest unappealing, even with the historically low levels of military spending, traditional military security may be more abundant than we recognise. This overabundance of traditional security, however, generates its own challenges, potentially tempting states to make mistakes while pursuing an elusive perfect security strategy. Washington's reaction to the September 2001 terrorist attacks, which over time arguably created far more misery and insecurity while undermining long-term US strategic interests, may be a case in point. And unlike in the age of scarcity, neither Russia nor China face any meaningful external threat to their survival or security.

Beyond issues of traditional security, states now also contend with collective-action issues, radical uncertainty, vexing externalities and the tragedy of the commons, as well as non-linear events and longer timelines. If states and international organisations remain focused on challenges from the past, if they govern and pursue foreign policy as if the danger remains scarcity, not plenty, then the grave and potentially catastrophic problems facing the world are unlikely to be effectively understood, let alone mitigated. As Veronica Anghel notes, the global COVID-19 pandemic revealed that many developed states with powerful militaries performed poorly against COVID-19, a problem of plenty, tallying 'human losses with equal grief to younger democracies with less resources and less celebrated forefathers'. For these new issues like climate change and cross-continent migration, traditional, nation-focused solutions that worked to conquer scarcity are, for the problems of plenty, 'more than ineffective, they are damaging'.[81]

New conceptual and intellectual lenses are needed to make sense of this new world of plenty. Realism and liberal internationalism, two powerful theories that help explain the past, are often challenged when asked to explain the present and future. Indeed, their key insights and recommendations could make things far worse. Realism makes sense of a disappearing world marked by scarcity, where territory was the key source of power, survival was uncertain and state conquest and empire-building were the norm. Coercion and offensive military power, the primary tools emphasised by realism, are not helpful to cool the planet, manage disinformation or halt a deadly pandemic – catastrophic threats far more pressing and existential than the unlikely rise of a new Eurasian hegemon. The insights provided by liberal internationalism are also limited. The institutions and practices that generated deeply integrated global markets and encouraged democratic convergence have created many of the problems of plenty that vex the current international system. While liberal international tools helped end great depressions, stabilise national and global politics, and generate collective security, they also helped cause crises ranging from climate change to disinformation to sociocultural fragmentation. They have not proven fit for purpose to deal with a world shaped by abundance.

To better grapple with these complex issues, analysts, scholars and policymakers need to move away from debates, methods and intellectual traditions that were developed for and appropriate to understanding the much different world of scarcity. They must also recognise that the problems of plenty are different in quality and character from those of scarcity. These problems are extraordinarily complex; they emerge, develop and interact in unexpected, non-linear ways, and are marked by unpredictable timelines. The novelty of these issues means the past cannot be used simply as direct precedent for what is likely to come. Unlike a great-power war, it can be hard to say anything definitively about the precise causes, timing or consequences of the problems of plenty, which is extremely disquieting. As one astute analyst notes, 'we know that we are headed in the wrong direction – the planet is heating up – but it remains unclear how far we have gone and how fast we are moving, especially when it comes to the impacts on planetary life'. In other words, the world faces radical uncertainty, where the kind of probabilistic predictions and theoretical generalisations that mark much previous policy and scholarly analysis may not provide much insight to the problems of plenty. No one, especially politicians, likes uncertainty. Yet as Geoff Mann suggests, 'we are in desperate need of a politics that looks catastrophic uncertainty square in the face'.[82]

V. American grand strategy in a world of plenty

The new shape, structure and incentives of the international system have profound implications for which policies and postures will be most effective in the years ahead. The transition from scarcity to plenty generates important, if contested, questions about the choices available to arguably the most consequential player in world politics, the US.

A key part of the debate over American grand strategy is shaped by how one views the causal drivers of the age of plenty. Did structural forces such as demographic, economic and technological revolutions transform the international system, or did grand-strategic choices by leading states drive the transition from scarcity to plenty? Specifically, was the United States' central role in constructing, maintaining and expanding a liberal world order after 1945 – in contrast to its choices after the First World War and earlier – crucial to this transition? If tectonic forces shape world politics, perhaps Washington's grand-strategic choices are less consequential.

But if the age of plenty was made possible by what some analysts characterise as America's far-sighted post-war hegemony, US leaders might look to maintain a US-dominated international environment.[83]

These are important questions that should be fiercely debated. Evaluating the role that US grand strategy played in fostering the change from scarcity to plenty will affect what you think it should do in the future. Some would argue that what they characterise as America's wise Cold War grand strategy – reflected in policies such as sponsoring the Bretton Woods institutions; offering Europe the Marshall Plan; creating NATO; encouraging decolonisation; and rehabilitating, pacifying, and becoming friends with former enemies like (West) Germany and Japan – was necessary to create the conditions that tamed scarcity, produced plenty and transformed world politics. Others might disagree. Plenty began with changes that occurred before the end of the Second World War. Though the greatest advancements took place in the twentieth century and accelerated in recent decades, the first elements of the modern agricultural revolution began much earlier, as did modern public-health measures, medical advances and reforms in governance.[84] Demographic compression in Europe, though unnoticed at the time, began during the late nineteenth century. Life-altering technologies ranging from electric refrigerators to televisions to automobiles became available before the Second World War. The length and quality of life and literacy were already expanding in the developed world, food and energy supplies increasing and remarkable new technologies emerging well before the US vigorously engaged the world. Very few of these breakthroughs were unleashed by any state's grand strategy, let alone America's. And many of the new aspects of plenty that emerged, deepened and accelerated after the Second World

War were only loosely connected, if at all, to America's behaviour in world politics.

Which view is correct? This question is very difficult to answer definitively, since evaluating these claims involves interrogating counterfactuals: assessing and reconstructing how the world might have changed, and the international system developed, if the US, or other leading actors, had made different choices. For example, it is possible to imagine another world emerging from plausible political alternatives: President Franklin D. Roosevelt retaining the progressive Henry Wallace, who sought friendly post-war relations with the Soviet Union, as his vice president in the 1944 election, instead of switching to Harry Truman; Robert Taft, an opponent of the US joining NATO, not Dwight D. Eisenhower, becoming the Republican Party's presidential nominee and winning the presidency in 1952; Richard Nixon winning the close election in 1960 or losing the equally close contest in 1968. If one or all of these alternative worlds had come to pass, the US might have pursued different policies and even grand strategies, with important consequences for world politics. There are also credible counterfactuals beyond the US. For example, if Social Democratic Party leader Kurt Schumacher had won the 1949 election in the new Federal Republic of Germany, as many expected, he may have made deep concessions to the Soviet Union, including offering neutrality and rejecting NATO, in order to unify Germany. The Cold War would have developed quite differently if that had occurred.

Similarly, many analysts attribute at least one aspect of plenty – increased security – primarily to the existence of thermonuclear weapons, which many believe prevented a third world war. Did nuclear weapons increase global peace, security and stability, creating the conditions for plenty to flower? Or did they generate great danger, near misses and nuclear crises, including the Taiwan Strait Crisis (1954–55), the Berlin Crises (1958–61), the Cuban Missile Crisis (1962) and the 1983 Able Archer affair, which might never have occurred in a non-nuclear world? In the emerging world of plenty, might the costs and incentives within the international system have shifted enough to dampen the drive for conquest and empire, even in a non-nuclear world, making total war increasingly unlikely? Again, answers are speculative, because the only historical evidence we have is of a post-war world with thermonuclear weapons. Indeed, the US could also have plausibly pursued very different grand strategies surrounding nuclear weapons – seeking nuclear disarmament or embracing a minimal deterrent, refusing to extend its nuclear umbrella to third parties, or being unconcerned with or even encouraging nuclear proliferation – which might have affected security in the world of plenty.

Calculating the precise interaction between structural forces and individual or national agency is difficult, contentious, and worthy of deeper exploration and debate. At least two features of the development of plenty, however, are certain. The profound changes in the length and quality of human life discussed above would have unfolded largely due to demographic, technological and socio-economic forces, regardless of what grand strategy the US chose, with great consequences for the international system. At the same time, the US, more than any other power, created the institutions, practices and norms that helped accelerate these powerful structural forces that tamed scarcity. The American-led liberal and security order deepened and spread the forces that increased the creation of wealth, information and security. And US grand strategy could influence how such material prosperity affected the nature of international relations.

The United States' accomplishments in driving plenty, however, were not entirely positive, for at least three reasons. Firstly, arguably no nation's policies or activities have contributed more to creating and worsening the potentially existential problems of plenty than the US. The American economy – and the liberal trading order it developed – has generated enormous planetary burdens, not the least of which is the disastrous climate crisis. America's digital-technology companies have, arguably, done more to facilitate widespread disinformation than any other global force. The US is burdened by steep inequality, and its commitment to foreign development aid meant to reduce global inequality is unimpressive.[85] It is also plagued by deeply polarised and fragmented domestic politics, preventing the nation or the government from generating a cohesive, vigorous shared vision. Arguably, much of the increased dissatisfaction with America's governance and institutions likely emerges from their inability to effectively deal with these new problems, which undermines their political legitimacy.

Secondly, for all its achievements, the American-led order that emerged to deal with scarcity is ill-suited to deal with the potentially catastrophic planetary challenges of plenty. Furthermore, by far the largest part of America's grand-strategic investment has been and remains in state tools – offensive military power – that were constructed to deal with and were ideal for an age of great-power total war but are far less helpful for confronting the problems brought by abundance.

To a certain extent, this is a puzzle. The 2022 US National Security Strategy recognises, correctly, that 'the climate crisis is the existential challenge of our time'.[86] Yet measured by resources, policies, rhetoric and political commitment, the US has a far greater focus on how to deal with traditional but decidedly non-existential issues, such as the rise and aggressiveness of the People's Republic of China (PRC). In truth, US grand strategy has failed to adjust to the transition from scarcity to plenty. Unlike in the past, territory is no longer the dominant source of power, empire is unattractive, there is little threat of a Eurasian hegemon, and the US will not be conquered, nor is it likely that its closest allies will be. Furthermore, climate change, pandemics, disinformation or inequality cannot be tackled by bombing or invasions.

Thirdly, in stark contrast to its role as a world leader in combatting scarcity, America has, to date, failed to demonstrate the urgency or necessary leadership to coordinate international action on the problems of plenty. While the Inflation Reduction Act (IRA) of 2022 was an impressive start to tackling these issues – though it was insufficient, and focused on national priorities over global coordination and cooperation – the US has not committed anywhere near enough resources for addressing these threats. Though there has been some improvement, America's level of political and socio-economic commitment to combatting the climate crisis is lower than that of most of its developed peers, and certainly comes nowhere near what is needed. It has regulated emerging technologies inconsistently. Even its most forward-leaning policies only confront its deep inequality at the margins. The economic dynamism and innovation that distinguishes the US from many other developed states, and which can serve as such a comparative advantage in the world of plenty, can often operate in tension with socio-economic equality. And most worryingly, its response to the global COVID-19 pandemic has been, over two presidential administrations, haphazard at best. While the US was a key player in the development of safe and effective vaccines, its death rate was higher than that of many nations that are far poorer and possess less advanced medical and public-health infrastructures.

The issue that does dominate American grand strategy, as well as analytical and scholarly debates surrounding it, is the challenge of China's rise and belligerence. How should the US deal with China in an age of plenty? This is another contentious issue, and attitudes about it often reflect views of the contemporary nature of world politics and the international system.

The CCP possesses a dreadful human-rights record, has brutally repressed its Uyghur minority and has squashed any hopes of democracy in its country. It has pursued predatory and unfair economic policies and demonstrated little respect for intellectual property. It has bullied its neighbours, from South Korea and Japan to the Philippines and India. The deadly COVID-19 pandemic originated in China, and its failure to properly report the outbreak or cooperate with other national and global health officials was reprehensible. Its efforts to intimidate Taiwan and those that would support it are deeply worrisome. Its crackdown on free expression in a once semi-autonomous Hong Kong reveals what would be in store for Taiwan if China succeeded in taking it.

On the other hand, while China is often a bad actor, the direct threat it poses to the US should not be overstated. Its claims to Taiwan, regardless of how Americans feel about the issue, have been almost universally and passionately supported by the PRC's leadership and the vast majority of its citizens for decades, a stance that would not shift if China suddenly became an open, liberal and otherwise cooperative democracy. Meanwhile, it has pursued a failing grand strategy of its own, with its increasingly bombastic manner managing to alienate countries near and far, while generating powerful balancing coalitions against it. It lacks true friends, reliable allies or attractive power, and its economy, facing massive debt and structural challenges, appears stalled. China spends enormous resources on its internal security.[87] The problems of plenty, such as the climate crisis, public-health emergencies, inequality and managing emerging technology, are likely to strike China harder than most. Its pandemic response was, to put it mildly, deeply flawed. The CCP is arguably doing more to undermine China's global position than any policy of the US.

Reasonable people can disagree on Washington's most effective grand-strategic response to deal with China. Standing up to bullies and punishing antediluvian efforts at conquest, be it Russia's reprehensible invasion of Ukraine or the PRC's coercion and threats against Taiwan, reflect deeply held, long-standing and admirable American values. Taiwan possesses an innovative economy, a thriving democracy and a robust civil society, and has made admirable choices under extreme pressure. And as Kori Schake reminds us, 'what motivates Americans to care about the world is values ... Americans want to defend religious and political liberty because it is who they are.'[88] It is not surprising that America's wariness and concern about China have increased in recent years.

That said, China does not represent an existential threat to the US in the age of plenty – far from it – nor should containing it be an organising principle of American grand strategy. Well-meaning hawks who suggest that it should be have not accounted for sharp differences between the Soviet Union during the Cold War and China today, the profound shifts in the nature of power and interest as the world has moved from scarcity to plenty, and how obsessing over the rivalry with China blinds the US to far more difficult, potentially existential challenges. China's desire for Taiwan is, in all likelihood, irredentist, or finite, as opposed to the open-ended imperialist ambitions that marked the age of scarcity. In the unlikely event that China's ambitions reach beyond irredentism to global domination, the fundamental shifts in the international system brought by plenty, combined with its own limitations, mean that it is very unlikely to achieve the kind of geopolitical power and imperial reach that Napoleon's France, the British Empire, Wilhelmine Germany, the Third Reich, Imperial Japan or the Soviet Union threatened (and ultimately failed to maintain) in a different era. In other words, there is little evidence that China wants an empire based on large-scale, open-ended imperial conquest; if it did, it is highly unlikely it could achieve it; and if it somehow managed to achieve it, it would likely guarantee its ruin.

When developing grand strategy towards China, Washington should recognise that the disagreement over Taiwan is the one issue that could cause an old-style great-power war between nuclear superpowers, which would be an unmitigated disaster for China, the US and the world. Other traditional issues, while generating sharp disagreements, do not represent the same level of danger.[89] American grand strategy could focus on the delicate and explosive Taiwan issue, and balance between competing forces and interests: recognising that the PRC and most of its population firmly believe its historical claims to Taiwan are valid and inviolable, while calling out and raising the costs of its effort to accomplish this end through unacceptable coercion and violence, and against the will of the people who live in Taiwan. Indeed, perhaps America's most successful grand-strategic policy over the past half-century has done just that, with the policies laid out in its Shanghai Communiqué and 'One China' policy, the Taiwan Relations Act, the Six Assurances and the Three No's.[90] Deterrence and assurance of both the PRC and Taiwan has, until recent years, worked, and should continue to guide America's policy over Taiwan. This policy has been shaken, not least by China's increasing threats, domestic repression and reckless behaviour abroad, which should be criticised and countered. It is important to remember, however, that the most likely alternatives to the past half-century of US policy on this issue are deeply troubling: a great-power war between two nuclear-armed states, or the conquest and possible suppression of the democratic Taiwanese population. Both prospects are appalling. The loss of Taiwan would entail steep costs, undermining America's position and deeply worrying US allies in the region, unsettling the global liberal order and upending life for the people of Taiwan. The US may reasonably decide, given these costs, that intervening in a conflict over Taiwan is necessary. The dangers of such a conflict, including the risk of a thermonuclear war, must always be kept in mind.

In an ideal but, at present, highly unlikely world, China and the US would coordinate and cooperate to mitigate and solve the problems of plenty that threaten both with catastrophe without either side being forced into unacceptable and humiliating concessions. The previously unimaginable tragedy of the COVID-19 pandemic that befell both countries – each with more than 1m dead – highlights the steep and often avoidable cost of the deep distrust and animosity between two great powers.[91] Similar and potentially more dangerous and lethal crises stemming from plenty appear inevitable, yet current circumstances make it hard to imagine how such cooperation would ever emerge, especially as the Taiwan challenge remains dangerous and unresolved. Still, such cooperation and coordination, which are clearly in both countries' best interests, should always be held up as a goal, even if an unattainable one.[92] And America's grand-strategic posture and policies should move away from rhetoric that implies, incorrectly, that the competition with China is generational, existential and civilisational – as opposed to the problems of plenty, which most decidedly are. While it can contest Chinese actions and resist its bad behaviour where necessary, it should avoid branding China's interests, even if disputed, as illegitimate, a framing that makes the grievous error that armed conflict between two nuclear superpowers is unavoidable.

There is a historical model to call upon, where bitter ideological and geopolitical adversaries worked together to solve problems of plenty. During the 1960s and 1970s, the US and the Soviet Union, despite their deep animosity and clash of values and interests, recognised their shared vulnerability and responsibility to each other and the planet to avoid nuclear war. They created a global regime to limit the spread of nuclear weapons, while also agreeing to temper the strategic arms competition between them. This grand-strategic impulse, contested and controversial when first pursued, was more successful than anyone could have imagined: 60 years ago, no one could have possibly hoped that the world today would contain only nine nuclear-weapons states and fewer nuclear weapons, or, most importantly, that the bomb had not been used again in a war.[93] Concurrently, these bitter rivals worked together to tame another deadly scourge: smallpox. This disease, which had tormented the world for centuries and killed as many as 2m people a year during the early 1960s – over the twentieth century accounting for twice as many people as died in warfare – was eliminated by the late 1970s, largely through the cooperative efforts of the Cold War adversaries.[94] These examples may perhaps seem naive and idealistic as models for contemporary cooperation, but the gulf between the Cold War superpowers was as wide, and arguably much wider, than that between China and the US today.

Three core principles for a new American grand strategy
Writ large, American grand strategy should be guided by three core principles.

Firstly, the US should recognise that the international system has been transformed, scarcity has largely been tamed and the problems of plenty are in the ascendant. It must do a better job of challenging unspoken assumptions, and avoiding historical time lags and anamnesis, while understanding that the world it faces now and in the years to come is much different to the one it confronted in earlier periods. By framing grand strategy and world politics solely through the lens of the past, while focusing on organising principles such as geopolitics, the return of great-power politics and a new Cold War, it risks, at best, misallocating resources, and at worst, courting disaster. This does not mean that war will disappear or that coercion is no longer an important grand-strategic tool. It does mean, however, that the greatest threats to the US and the international system include a melting planet and the dangers that come with it, destabilising new technologies, and the cancer of inequality, deep polarisation, and sociocultural fragmentation and alienation, but not the unlikely emergence of an expanding industrial, mobilised Eurasian hegemon. The states that best adapt to this new world of plenty, and recognise, produce and employ more effective types of power, will thrive.

Secondly, the US should thoughtfully examine the institutions, policies and practices that helped tame scarcity. It should continue to support and strengthen efforts to create more wealth, generate collective security and deepen knowledge of the world, with an eye towards more fairly spreading the benefits of plenty at home and to people and parts of the world that have not yet fully profited. It must do so, however, while vigorously attending to and limiting those aspects of increased prosperity that deepen the problems of plenty. In particular, it must prioritise limiting the amount of carbon released into the atmosphere, confront the deep domestic and global inequalities generated by plenty, and face and regulate the dangers brought by new technologies, especially disinformation. In other words, it must do a better job of reaping the benefits of plenty while mitigating its harms.

Thirdly, the US should lead efforts to develop innovative institutions, policies and practices to deal with the new world of abundance. This will be difficult: modern structures of government, both on the national and the international level, were intended predominantly to solve the problems of scarcity in a world where the memory of conquest and total war was ever present. Much of this organisational scaffolding is outdated or poorly suited to solving the problems of plenty. Whereas the problems of scarcity demanded mass mobilisation and unity of purpose, and that governments focused on offensive military power, tackling the problems of plenty requires nimbleness, innovation, diversity, transparency, adaptability and accountability to be effective and maintain governmental legitimacy. When constructing these institutions and policies, lessons could be applied from successful private-sector firms, with their ability to rapidly adapt and self-correct when circumstances change. In other instances, the achievements of non-governmental entities such as the Gates Foundation, with a focus on metrics to measure success and incentives to shift behaviour, will provide a model. Other problems will demand that governments construct and lead partnerships that include both governmental and non-governmental institutions. This will require deep cooperation and coordination across sectors and among states – conditions that are very difficult to achieve. PEPFAR, mentioned earlier, is one successful example. Another is the combination of private-sector finance, technological innovation and government incentives in driving an energy transition in the US. According to Goldman Sachs, the US is currently experiencing 'a third energy revolution' whereby the amount of energy produced by 'solar, wind, electric vehicles (EVs), and storage, as well as bio-energy, clean hydrogen, and carbon capture' will dwarf what is currently provided by fossil fuels by 2050.[95] In most cases, attraction will often be more effective than coercion; ideas more critical than territory. Most importantly, the problems of plenty often are extraordinarily complex and difficult to manage, being issues of the commons that transcend territorial borders and do not lend themselves to zero-sum or easily defined equilibrium solutions. The problems of plenty often operate along longer time horizons that are out of sync with how, when and why most political (and non-governmental) institutions react.

Given that the US faces deep political polarisation and grand-strategic anamnesis, are there reasons to believe it can update, improve and transform its grand strategies to better meet the problems of plenty? There is cause for optimism. The US enjoys qualities that may have been less relevant to power in a world of scarcity but could provide benefits in a world of plenty, including decentralised political power; great research universities; disaggregated national identity; geographical breadth; population diversity and ease of movement (without a dominating national metropole); the ability to attract and assimilate ideas, practices and talent from abroad; and a strong and impressive private and non-profit sector.

The problems of plenty are daunting. But so were the problems of scarcity, which were largely tamed in the developed world. The principles and lessons from both nuclear-arms control and smallpox eradication reveal that, with enough political leadership, vision and will, even the bitterest of enemies can work together to contain planetary challenges.

Conclusion

'The condition of man', claimed Thomas Hobbes in his 1651 classic *Leviathan*, 'is a condition of war of everyone against everyone'. His description of the human condition in the state of nature forms the bedrock of the most important school of international relations, realism.

> Cities and kingdoms ... enlarge their own dominions, upon all pretenses of danger, and fear of invasion, or assistance that may be given to invaders, endeavour as much as they can, to subdue, or weaken their neighbours, by open force, and secret arts, for want of other caution, justly; and are remembered for it in after ages with honour.[96]

Hobbes based these insights on his personal experience, writing in the context of a series of brutal and bloody civil wars in England, Scotland and Ireland.

Conflict and hardship were not limited to the British Isles, however. States and empires around the world in the seventeenth century, and especially the generations between the late 1610s and the 1680s, witnessed horrific global catastrophes – war, revolution, famine, disease, repression, mass imposition of slavery, even increased suicides – that killed up to one-third of the human population. New historical research has identified the key cause: climate change. As Geoffrey Parker has explained, 'demographers and climatologists suggest that around 1618, when the human population of the northern hemisphere was larger than ever before, the average global temperature started to fall, producing extreme climate events, disastrous harvest failures and frequent disease epidemics'. Instead of trying to deal with these environmental dangers with prudent strategies, 'most governments around the globe exacerbated the situation by continuing their existing policies, above all their wars'.[97] This period of intense crisis only ended when, by the end of the century, the climate had stabilised and the massively reduced human population found equilibrium with available resources, dramatically reducing conflict while restoring political stability. This history is a reminder that Hobbes was not simply a father of realism. Knowingly or not, *Leviathan* is also an account of how changes in the earth's climate, combined with misguided political responses to the challenges this presents, generate profound consequences for the human condition and the international system.

Hobbes's world and our own share a similar vulnerability to the environment. His insights into the motivating role fear plays in human behaviour also remain valid. But the source and immediacy of much of that fear has changed because of the subsequent taming of scarcity and the emergence of plenty. The differences between the world of his day and today are profound. Much of man's individual and collective effort since Hobbes's time has been devoted to escaping human exposure to the natural world – taking advantage of the earth's resources to generate enough wealth, knowledge and safety so that we could feed, clothe, house and protect ourselves regardless of the climate or other variables and, in doing so, leave behind the scarcity that had long afflicted human existence. Remarkably, the developed world has succeeded in this task beyond what anyone in Hobbes's time could have imagined, generating previously unfathomable amounts of economic resources, information and security. Numerous ills that once plagued humanity have been tamed, humans live twice as long and in far greater comfort and safety, and violence of all types has fallen. In the process, a key driver of states and empires embarking upon great-power war – pursuing or protecting themselves from plunder, territorial expansion and imperial conquest – no longer makes political or socio-economic sense in a world of plenty.

Unfortunately, in accomplishing these extraordinary feats, man has unleashed novel, potentially existential dangers – the problems of plenty – which threaten human life on the planet. Our very economic success – and excess – may make large parts of the earth increasingly uninhabitable. The unjust way we distribute this bounty fosters destabilising bitterness, anger and resentment. The new, powerful technologies we have invented may create unknown but existential consequences. Access to all the world's information often leaves us overwhelmed, paralysed and polarised, unclear as to what is true and what is a lie. The search for an unattainable perfect security may lull us into calamitous wars that serve little purpose.

There are two obvious critiques of this argument. Firstly, has scarcity truly been tamed? Indeed, poverty, insecurity and misery still menace far too many people around the world who lack predictable food supplies, access to clean water and medicine, education and personal safety. This is tragic and unforgivable because, unlike in the past, *we possess the means and the know-how to tame scarcity*. It should be a goal of the developed world, and especially the US, to help disseminate the benefits of plenty – wealth, knowledge and security – to those who are currently left out, while minimising or mitigating the tragic problems that come with it. This goal is particularly urgent as the problems of plenty are largely generated by the US and the developed world, yet unfairly most threaten the vulnerable citizens of poorer regions and countries, who are least able to cope and adapt.

The second critique involves claims about the transformed nature of the international system. Does Russia's brutal invasion of, and effort to conquer, Ukraine, for example, not disprove the core argument of this essay – that conquest and imperial aggression are acts from the past?

In fact, the war in Ukraine is the exception that proves the rule. It is hard to imagine that any other great power assesses Russia's decision to invade Ukraine as a wise grand-strategic move they seek to emulate. Regardless of the ultimate outcome of the war, it seems clear that Russia's power position will be degraded for decades to come; its military forces greatly diminished; its economy shrunken and increasingly cut off from the developed world; its international reputation in tatters; and many of its smartest, best citizens permanently moved abroad. It now depends almost entirely upon China, a historical rival, and unsavoury regimes like Iran and North Korea to sustain its war effort, all while the NATO alliance it faces has expanded and strengthened. It has paid and will continue to pay a steep price for its brutal and stupid behaviour. Why should any other power think similar efforts would turn out better?

One reason that events such as Russia's invasion, or Hamas's brutal pogrom against Israeli civilians of late 2023, are so shocking is that such events have been increasingly rare in the era of plenty. We have forgotten that war, mass killings and conquest were ubiquitous in international life not so long ago. Consider just one example, proximate to the conflict in Ukraine. The war between Poland and the Soviet Union in 1919–21 caused more than 350,000 casualties, including over 100,000 deaths. Yet conflict was so prevalent in the past that this war is unknown by most and rarely commented upon, or, when it is acknowledged, it is often subsumed within the Russian civil war, a distinct catastrophe that killed between 7m and 12m people. Neither is it pointed out that during the same period, while one combatant, the

Soviet Union, was prosecuting an unimaginably murderous civil war, the other, the newly independent state of Poland, was at war, off and on, over territory with its neighbours Czechoslovakia, Germany, Latvia, Lithuania and Ukraine. Or that contemporaneously in Ukraine, at least 100,000 Jews were targeted and killed in pogroms, many state sponsored. The 'interwar' period is often thought of as a peaceful if tense interlude between two global conflagrations, but in fact it was marked by brutal conflict in every part of the globe. War, imperialism, revolution and wholescale slaughter of innocents were horrifyingly commonplace in the past. The fortunately exceptional rarity of these tragedies in the age of plenty, at least in the developed world and compared to the era of scarcity, understandably generates greater outrage and a more robust response.

This raises another question: if we are in a new world, with new forms of power and a transformed international system, facing planetary threats that demand innovative, coopera-tive and non-coercive responses, why do some (though not most) developed states, particularly the US, view the war in Ukraine, in addition to a looming conflict with China, as the correct organising principle for world politics and their own grand strategies?

As this essay has made clear, war will not go away, coercion remains a necessary tool, and China's rise and belligerence presents important though certainly not existential, civili-sational or generational challenges. Part of the explanation, however, lies in historical time lags, unspoken assumptions and historical anamnesis: states and people rarely recog-nise, in real time (or before it is too late), that their world has changed, nor do they easily develop the new conceptual lenses, institutions, policies and processes that are needed to thrive and survive. States – and people – rely on muscle memory to solve problems, revealing the natural, status quo bias that individuals and institutions possess. This is especially true in the US, where its sprawling institutions and processes – from the national-security bureaucracy to how international relations is taught and researched in higher education – were organised to understand and navigate a different era, the world of scarcity. The existing institutional apparatus helped America win the Second World War and outlast the Soviet Union during the Cold War: remarkable achievements. This apparatus has been largely impotent against the potentially existential threats that will dominate the future. As the United States' ineffectual response to the COVID-19, climate and opioid crises reveal, America possesses neither the conceptual nor the institutional tools to understand, let alone tackle, the problems of plenty. This is not just a problem among professors and policymakers, as the American public's disappointing responses reveal. The fastest-growing cities in the US include Austin, Miami and Phoenix, areas where scorching temperatures are rising to unliveable levels, and which will either run out of or be under water before long.

The truth is that the problems of plenty are very difficult to satisfactorily understand and analyse, let alone solve. Great-power wars are horrific but there is a sense of, if not a consensus on, why they occur and how they unfold. In the fifth century BCE, Thucydides argued that war was motivated by 'fear, honour and interest'. Not much has changed in the centuries since, although the way contemporary states define their interests has shifted enormously. The problems of plenty, in contrast, confound us by their very complexity, interconnectedness and non-linear patterns. The past cannot provide a simple road map for this new world and, unless carefully handled, history is just as likely to mislead as instruct. In this context, historical understanding serves an indispensable function by revealing how the current, and likely future, world differs so powerfully from that of the past. That has been one of the goals of this essay.

Most unsettling, these problems confront us with radical uncertainty; we have no idea what the future holds. Perhaps we will develop technological and political solutions to climate and technology challenges and the crises will abate. Or perhaps we are in an inevitable doom spiral towards catastrophe and human extinction that we cannot stop. We do not even know how to think about, let alone measure, the 'tail risks' – the unlikely but dramatic outcomes. This lack of knowledge makes these challenges especially daunting and unsettling. The characteristics of the problems of plenty lend themselves to the precautionary principle – where the potential threats are so catastrophic that we should not allow their unpredictability or our deep uncertainty to inhibit a vigorous policy response – that is often at odds with how much of the developed world's political and policy processes operate.

Not to put too fine a point on the current challenge: imagine, a century from now, a world that had suffered from innumerable, cascading and mutually reinforcing problems of plenty. The consequence of these challenges being unmet would probably be that our descendants would no longer be living on the treasure island of the developed world today, or even our ancestors' desert island marked by scarcity, but something closer to a 'deathly island' – sterile and soon to sink underwater. Should anyone still be alive on the overheated, desiccated planet, they might emerge from their underground bunkers struggling to make sense of why we did not do more to prepare for the coming apocalyptic world when there was still a chance to make a difference, and trying to comprehend why leading thinkers of our time were still discussing the return of great-power competition or regur-gitating the works of geopolitical thinkers like Mahan and Mackinder in order to control dying oceans or uninhabitable land. But this deathly future is not inevitable. We can, in fact, think more clearly. We must do so if we hope to survive.

NOTES

1   There is, of course, a spirited debate
    among political philosophers
    concerning the state of nature
    and human circumstances in
    early societies. For a fascinating
    anthropological view that argues
    hunter-gatherers were the original
    affluent society, 'in which all the
    people's material wants are easily
    satisfied', a claim that denies that
    'the human condition is an ordained
    tragedy, with man the prisoner at
    hard labor of a perpetual disparity
    between his unlimited wants and
    his insufficient means', see Marshall
    D. Sahlins, *Stone Age Economics*
    (Abingdon: Routledge, 1972), p. 1.

2   Norman Angell, *The Great Illusion:
    A Study of the Relation of Military
    Power in Nations to Their Economic
    and Social Advantage* (New York and
    London: G.P. Putnam's Sons, 1911).

3   Adam Tooze, 'Welcome to the
    World of the Polycrisis', *Financial
    Times*, 28 October 2022, https://
    www.ft.com/content/498398e7-11b1-
    494b-9cd3-6d669dc3de33.

4   Saloni Dattani et al., 'Life
    Expectancy', Our World in Data,
    https://ourworldindata.org/life-
    expectancy.

5   'Burundi – Life Expectancy at Birth',
    countryeconomy.com, https://
    countryeconomy.com/demography/
    life-expectancy/burundi.

6   Max Roser and Esteban Ortiz-
    Ospina, 'Literacy', Our World in
    Data, 20 September 2018, https://
    ourworldindata.org/literacy.

7   US Department of Agriculture
    Economic Research Service, 'Feeding
    the World: Global Food Production
    Per Person Has Grown Over
    Time', 13 November 2023, https://
    www.ers.usda.gov/data-products/
    chart-gallery/gallery/chart-
    detail/?chartId=107818#:~:text=Fe
    eding%20the%20world%3A%20
    Global%20food,increased%20
    13%20percent%20on%20average;
    and 'Daily Support of Calories per
    Person, 2018', Our World in Data,
    https://ourworldindata.org/grapher/
    daily-per-capita-caloric-supply.

8   Mike Davis, *Late Victorian Holocausts: El Niño Famines and the Making of the Third World* (London: Verso, 2001), p. 7. India's famine during the Second World War claimed three million lives, and anywhere from 17m to 45m died during the Great Leap Forward in China in 1959–61. There is disagreement about the relative importance of food and information scarcity on the one hand and the role of malign political forces on the other in these catastrophes.

9   Naomi Williams and Graham Mooney, 'Infant Mortality in an "Age of Great Cities": London and the English Provincial Cities Compared, c. 1840–1910', *Continuity and Change*, vol. 9, no. 2, August 1994, pp. 185–212.

10 Claude Fischer, 'A Crime Puzzle: Violent Crime Declines in America', *Berkeley News*, 16 June 2010, https://news.berkeley.edu/2010/06/16/a-crime-puzzle-violent-crime-declines-in-america/; and Kristin Englund, 'Syphilis 100 Years Later', Cleveland Clinic, 21 November 2017, https://consultqd.clevelandclinic.org/syphilis-100-years-later/.

11 William H. McNeill, *Population and Politics Since 1750* (Charlottesville, VA: University of Virginia Press, 1990), p. 1.

12 For two of the more important works on the causes of war, see Jack S. Levy and William R. Thompson, *Causes of War* (Chichester: Wiley-Blackwell, 2010); and Stephen Van Evera, *Causes of War: Power and the Roots of Conflict* (Ithaca, NY and London: Cornell University Press, 1999).

13 John A. Vasquez, *The War Puzzle* (Cambridge: Cambridge University Press, 1993), pp. 151, 293, cited in John Mueller, 'War Has Almost Ceased to Exist: An Assessment', *Political Science Quarterly*, vol. 124, no. 2, Summer 2009, pp. 297–321 at 306–7.

14 T.R. Malthus, *An Essay on the Principle of Population* (Mineola, NY: Dover Publications, 2007 [1798]), p. 5.

15 United States Census Bureau, 'Historical Estimates of World Population', https://www.census.gov/data/tables/time-series/demo/international-programs/historical-est-worldpop.html.

16 Geoffrey Parker, *Global Crisis: War, Climate Change and Catastrophe in the Seventeenth Century* (New Haven, CT: Yale University Press, 2013), p. 25. The terms 'rebalancing' and 'equilibrium' are McNeill's.

17 *Ibid.*, p. 55.

18 *Ibid.*, p. 77.

19 'Population Change', Britannica, https://www.britannica.com/topic/modernization/Population-change.

20 John Burnett, 'Housing and the Decline of Mortality', in Roger Schofield, David Reher and Alain Bideau (eds), *The Decline of Mortality in Europe* (Oxford: Clarendon Press, 1991), pp. 158–76.

21 Jörg Vögele, 'Urbanization, Infant Mortality and Public Health in Imperial Germany', in Carlo A. Corsini and Pier Paolo Viazzo (eds), *The Decline of Infant and Child Mortality: The European Experience, 1750–1990* (The Hague: Martinus Nijhoff, 1997), p. 110.

22 McNeill, *Population and Politics Since 1750*, p. 51.

23 *Ibid.*, p. 24.

24 William H. McNeill, *The Pursuit of Power* (Chicago, IL: University

of Chicago Press, 1982), p. 310.
Population pressures in eighteenth-century China drove similar expansion, launching 'a vigorous and successful expansion across every landward frontier'. Settlers 'followed in the wake of the armies wherever suitable land existed', but after 1797 China faced both domestic and international restraints, causing it to descend into a century of 'civil strife' and increasing exposure to foreign domination. *Ibid.*, pp. 36–7.

25 *Ibid.*, p. 39.

26 Alison Bashford, *Global Population: History, Geopolitics, and Life on Earth* (New York: Columbia University Press, 2014).

27 Alison Bashford, 'Population Politics Since 1750', in J.R. McNeill and Kenneth Pomeranz (eds), *The Cambridge World History, Volume VII: Production, Destruction, and Connection, 1750–Present; Part 1: Structures, Spaces, and Boundary Making* (Cambridge: Cambridge University Press, 2015), pp. 222–3.

28 James Joll, '1914: The Unspoken Assumptions: An Inaugural Lecture Delivered 25 April 1968' (London: London School of Economics and Political Science, Weidenfeld and Nicolson, 1968), p. 23.

29 Avner Offer, *The First World War: An Agrarian Interpretation* (Oxford: Clarendon Press, 1989), pp. 8–9.

30 Steven Johnson, 'How Humanity Gave Itself an Extra Life', *New York Times*, 27 April 2021, https://www.nytimes.com/2021/04/27/magazine/global-life-span.html.

31 Ansley J. Coale, 'The Decline of Fertility in Europe Since the Eighteenth Century as a Chapter in Human Demographic History',
in Ansley J. Coale and Susan C. Watkins (eds), *The Decline of Fertility in Europe: The Revised Proceedings of a Conference on the Princeton European Fertility Project* (Princeton, NJ: Princeton University Press, 1986), pp. 1–30.

32 Paul Morland, *The Human Tide: How Population Shaped the Modern World* (New York: Public Affairs, 2019), pp. 11–68.

33 Ansley J. Coale and Roy Treadway, 'A Summary of the Changing Distribution of Overall Fertility, Marital Fertility, and the Proportion Married in the Provinces of Europe', in Coale and Watkins (eds), *The Decline of Fertility in Europe*, pp. 31–181.

34 Jennifer D. Sciubba, 'Intergenerational Controversy and Cultural Clashes: Political Consequences of Demographic Change in the US and Canada Since 1990', in Achim Goerres and Pieter Vanhuysse (eds), *Global Political Demography: The Politics of Population Change* (Cham, Switzerland: Springer International Publishing, 2021), pp. 325–50.

35 Damien Cave, Emma Bubola and Choe Sang-Hun, 'Long Slide Looms for World Population, With Sweeping Ramifications', *New York Times*, 22 May 2021, https://www.nytimes.com/2021/05/22/world/global-population-shrinking.html.

36 McNeill, *Population and Politics Since 1750*, p. 67.

37 Henrik Urdal, 'Youth Bulges and Violence', in Jack A. Goldstone, Eric P. Kaufmann and Monica Duffy Toft (eds), *Political Demography: How Population Changes Are Reshaping International Security*

and National Politics (New York: Oxford University Press, 2011), p. 123; Henrik Urdal, 'A Clash of Generations? Youth Bulges and Political Violence', *International Studies Quarterly*, vol. 50, no. 3, September 2006, pp. 607–29, cited in Morland, *The Human Tide*, p. 21; and Herbert Moller, 'Youth as a Force in the Modern World', *Comparative Studies in Society and History*, vol. 10, no. 3, 1968, pp. 237–60, cited in Morland, *The Human Tide*, p. 21.

38   Ronald Findlay and Kevin H. O'Rourke, *Power and Plenty: Trade, War, and the World Economy in the Second Millennium* (Princeton, NJ: Princeton University Press, 2007), pp. 515–16.

39   In current US dollars. See 'World GDP per Capita 1960–1924', macrotrends, https://www.macrotrends.net/countries/WLD/world/gdp-per-capita.

40   William N. Parker, 'Productivity Growth in American Grain Farming: An Analysis of Its Nineteenth Century Sources', in Robert W. Fogel and Stanley L. Engerman (eds), *The Reinterpretation of American Economic History* (New York: Harper and Row Publishers, 1971), p. 176. See also Scott R. Nelson, *Oceans of Grain: How American Wheat Remade the World* (New York: Hachette Group, 2022).

41   Philip G. Pardey and Julian M. Alston, 'The Drivers of U.S. Agricultural Productivity Growth', in Federal Reserve Bank of Kansas City, '2020 Agricultural Symposium: The Roots of Agricultural Productivity Growth', https://www.kansascityfed.org/documents/7107/the-drivers-of-us-agricultural-productivity-growth.pdf.

42   Vaclav Smil, *Enriching the Earth: Fritz Haber, Carl Bosch, and the Transformation of World Food Production* (London: MIT Press, 2001), p. 204.

43   Adam Tooze, 'Chartbook on Shutdown: Keynes and Why We Can Afford Anything We Can Do', Chartbook, 1 September 2021, https://adamtooze.substack.com/p/chartbook-on-shutdown-keynes-and.

44   Nadège Mougel, 'World War I Casualties', 2011, https://www.census.gov/history/pdf/reperes112018.pdf.

45   'World War II Fatalities by Country', WorldAtlas, https://www.worldatlas.com/world-wars/world-war-ii-fatalities-by-country.html.

46   Mueller, 'War Has Almost Ceased to Exist'.

47   Crystal Cazier and Andrew Kaufmann, 'An Oral History of PEPFAR', George W. Bush Presidential Center, 24 February 2023, https://www.bushcenter.org/publications/an-oral-history-of-pepfar-how-a-dream-big-partnership-is-saving-the-lives-of-millions.

48   Nils Petter Gleditsch et al., 'The Decline of War', *International Studies Review*, vol. 15, no. 3, September 2013, pp. 396–419. No one disputes that the number of great-power wars has declined since 1945 nor that the percentage of people likely to die in war is historically low. There is argument over the causes of these trends, whether they will continue or reverse, and how broadly or narrowly to define war.

49   Emily Elhacham et al., 'Global Human-made Mass Exceeds All Living Biomass', *Nature*, vol. 588,

no. 7838, December 2020, pp. 442–4, https://doi.org/10.1038/s41586-020-3010-5.

50 Martin McGuigan, 'The 6th Mass Extinction Hasn't Begun Yet, Study Claims, but Earth Is Barreling Toward It', *Live Science*, 11 August 2022, https://www.livescience.com/sixth-mass-extinction-underway/.

51 Jonathan S. Blake and Nils Gilman, *Children of a Modest Star: Planetary Thinking for an Age of Crises* (Redwood City, CA: Stanford University Press, forthcoming 2024), p. 17.

52 Margaret Osborne, 'Carbon Dioxide Levels Now Higher Than Ever in Human History', *Smithsonian Magazine*, 10 June 2022, https://www.smithsonianmag.com/smart-news/carbon-dioxide-levels-now-higher-than-ever-in-human-history-180980229/.

53 Robert Lee Hotz and Timothy Puko, 'Some Climate Change Effects May Be Irreversible, U.N. Panel Says', *Wall Street Journal*, 9 August 2021, https://www.wsj.com/articles/some-climate-change-effects-may-be-irreversible-u-n-panel-report-says-11628496000.

54 Blake and Gilman, *Children of a Modest Star*, p. 108.

55 Pamela Falk, 'Earth Just Had Its Hottest Summer on Record, U.N. Says, Warning "Climate Breakdown Has Begun"', CBS News, 7 September 2023, https://www.cbsnews.com/news/hottest-summer-on-record-2023-un-says-climate-change-global-warming-data/.

56 Ian Livingston, 'Hot-tub-like Persian Gulf Fuels 158-degree Heat Index in Iran', *Washington Post*, 9 August 2023, https://www.washingtonpost.com/weather/2023/08/09/iran-persian-gulf-extreme-heat/.

57 Lee Hotz and Puko, 'Some Climate Change Effects May Be Irreversible, U.N. Panel Says'.

58 Joshua M. Pearce and Richard Parncutt, 'Quantifying Global Greenhouse Gas Emissions in Human Deaths to Guide Energy Policy', *Energies*, vol. 16, no. 16, 2023, https://doi.org/10.3390/en16166074.

59 Ville Lähde, 'The Polycrisis', *Aeon*, 17 August 2023, https://aeon.co/essays/the-case-for-polycrisis-as-a-keyword-of-our-interconnected-times.

60 Kate Mackenzie and Tim Sahay, 'Global Boiling', The Polycrisis, 3 August 2023, https://www.phenomenalworld.org/analysis/global-boiling/.

61 Joe Zadeh, 'Concrete Built the Modern World. Now It's Destroying It', *Noema Magazine*, 6 December 2022, https://www.noemamag.com/concrete-built-the-modern-world-now-its-destroying-it/.

62 *Ibid.*

63 For suggestions on minimising these dangers, see Henry A. Kissinger and Graham Allison, 'The Path to AI Arms Control: America and China Must Work Together to Avert Catastrophe', *Foreign Affairs*, 13 October 2023, https://www.foreignaffairs.com/united-states/henry-kissinger-path-artificial-intelligence-arms-control.

64 Arden Koehler and Benjamin Hilton, 'Preventing Catastrophic Pandemics', 80,000 Hours blog, April 2020, updated July 2022, https://80000hours.org/problem-profiles/preventing-catastrophic-pandemics/.

65 Fyodor Urnov et al., 'Don't Edit the Human Germ Line', *Nature*, vol. 519, no. 7544, March 2015, pp. 410–11.

66 Trevor Johnston, Troy D. Smith and J. Luke Irwin, *Additive Manufacturing in 2040: Powerful Enabler, Disruptive Threat* (Santa Monica, CA: RAND Corporation, 2018), https://www.rand.org/pubs/perspectives/PE283.html.

67 Zia Qureshi, 'Rising Inequality: A Major Issue of Our Time', Brookings Institution, 16 May 2023, https://www.brookings.edu/articles/rising-inequality-a-major-issue-of-our-time/.

68 Blake and Gilman, *Children of a Modest Star*, p. 11.

69 Dirk Helbing, 'Globally Networked Risks and How to Respond', *Nature*, vol. 497, no. 7447, May 2013, pp. 51–9, https://doi.org/10.1038/nature12047.

70 Henry A. Kissinger, 'How the Enlightenment Ends', *The Atlantic*, June 2018, https://www.theatlantic.com/magazine/archive/2018/06/henry-kissinger-ai-could-mean-the-end-of-human-history/559124/.

71 Ian Bremmer and Mustafa Suleyman, 'The AI Power Paradox: Can States Learn to Govern Artificial Intelligence – Before It's Too Late?', *Foreign Affairs*, September/October 2023, https://www.foreignaffairs.com/world/artificial-intelligence-power-paradox.

72 Joshua Rovner, 'Information Overload and International Order', unpublished memo for the Ax:son Johnson Institute for Statecraft and Diplomacy Workshop on World Order, Bologna, Italy, 13 October 2023.

73 Mackenzie and Sahay, 'Global Boiling'.

74 'The Pandemic's True Death Toll', *The Economist*, 18 November 2023, https://www.economist.com/graphic-detail/coronavirus-excess-deaths-estimates.

75 As Jonathan Kirshner suggests, 'China would prove almost unimaginably hard to conquer' and its survival does not depend upon 'the military conquest of others', many of whom have nuclear weapons or could develop them quickly if threatened. Nor is the survival of the 'preternaturally secure United States' threatened by China. Indeed, the only thing that could threaten their survival is if they went to war with each other. Jonathan Kirshner, 'Addressing the China Challenge: Realisms Right and Wrong', *Los Angeles Review of Books*, 2 October 2023, https://lareviewofbooks.org/article/addressing-the-china-challenge-realisms-right-and-wrong/.

76 Paul Kennedy, *The Rise and Fall of the Great Powers* (New York: Penguin Random House, 1989), p. 85.

77 'U.S. Defense Spending Compared to Other Countries', Peter G. Peterson Foundation, 24 April 2023, https://www.pgpf.org/chart-archive/0053_defense-comparison#:~:text=Defense%20spending%20accounts%20for%2012,of%20the%20annual%20federal%20budget.

78 Pavel Luzin and Alexandra Prokopenko, 'Russia's 2024 Budget Shows It's Planning for a Long War in Ukraine', 11 October 2023, Carnegie Endowment for International Peace, https://carnegieendowment.org/politika/90753.

79 Joll, '1914: The Unspoken Assumptions', p. 6.

80 Jordan Schneider and Matthew
    Mittelsteadt, 'The Key to Winning
    the Global AI Race', *Noema Magazine*,
    19 September 2023, https://www.
    noemamag.com/the-key-to-winning-
    the-global-ai-race/.

81 Veronica Anghel, 'Anti-Virus
    Measures in European States Show
    the Weaknesses of Nation-States',
    Medium, 23 April 2020,
    https://medium.com/freeman-spogli-
    institute-for-international-studies/
    anti-virus-measures-in-european-
    states-show-the-weaknesses-of-
    nation-states-101d21c0fac2.

82 Geoff Mann, 'Treading Thin Air: Geoff
    Mann on Uncertainty and Climate
    Change', *London Review of Books*, vol.
    45, no. 17, 7 September 2023.

83 G. John Ikenberry, *Liberal Leviathan:
    The Origins, Crisis, and Transformation
    of the American World Order*
    (Princeton, NJ: Princeton University
    Press, 2011).

84 Theodore H. Tulchinsky and Elena
    A. Varavikova, 'A History of Public
    Health', in Theodore H. Tulchinsky
    and Elena A. Varavikova, *The New
    Public Health* (Cambridge, MA:
    Academic Press, 2014), pp. 1–42,
    https://doi.org/10.1016/B978-0-12-
    415766-8.00001-X.

85 The US provides less than 0.2% of
    its GDP in aid to poor countries, one
    of the lowest percentages among
    wealthy countries. See George
    Ingram, 'What Every American
    Should Know About US Foreign
    Aid', 2 October 2019, Brookings
    Institution, https://www.brookings.
    edu/articles/what-every-american-
    should-know-about-u-s-foreign-aid/.

86 The White House, 'National
    Security Strategy', 12 October 2022,
    p. 27, https://www.whitehouse.
    gov/wp-content/uploads/2022/10/
    Biden-Harris-Administrations-
    National-Security-Strategy-10.2022.
    pdf.

87 Michael Beckley, 'China's Century?
    Why America's Edge Will Endure',
    International Security, vol. 36, no. 3,
    Winter 2011–12, pp. 41–78.

88 Kori Schake, 'Can the US Make
    the World Safe for Democracy?',
    Engelsberg Ideas, 26 September
    2023, https://engelsbergideas.com/
    essays/can-the-us-make-the-world-
    safe-for-democracy/.

89 The US should always call out
    human-rights violations wherever
    they occur. It should also push
    back against China's mercantilist
    economic policies. While the US
    and its allies should continue to
    resist China's efforts at a 'Monroe
    Doctrine' in its region, they should
    be aware of why China would see
    those efforts as highly hypocritical
    coming from American officials.
    And having alienated much of the
    developed world through its inept
    grand strategy, China's efforts to
    either influence the current world
    order or create a new one are
    increasingly focused on the Global
    South, areas that have not fully
    participated in the benefits of plenty
    but are incurring many of its costs.
    The US and the developed world
    might learn something from this
    effort and also turn greater attention
    to that part of the world. See James
    Kynge, 'China's Blueprint for an
    Alternative World Order', *Financial
    Times*, 22 August 2023, https://www.
    ft.com/content/8ac52fe7-e9db-48a8-
    b2f0-7305ab53f4c3.

90 For the details of official policy
    statements in each relevant capital,

see 'China/Taiwan: Evolution of the "One China" Policy – Key Statements from Washington, Beijing, and Taipei', 5 January 2015, https://www.everycrsreport.com/reports/RL30341.html.

91 China may have lost almost 1.5m people in just three months – December 2022 to February 2023 – while the US death toll was over 1m, numbers that rival total wars between great powers in the past. For China, see Zhanwei Du et al., 'Estimate of COVID-19 Deaths, China, December 2022–February 2023', *Emerging Infectious Diseases*, vol. 29, no. 10, October 2023, https://doi.org/10.3201/eid2910.230585. For US figures, see Centers for Disease Control and Prevention, 'COVID Data Tracker', https://covid.cdc.gov/covid-data-tracker/#datatracker-home.

92 Interestingly, although China and the US have not fully cooperated when faced with global financial and monetary crises in recent decades, neither have they worked at cross purposes.

93 Francis J. Gavin, 'Strategies of Inhibition: U.S. Grand Strategy, the Nuclear Revolution, and Nonproliferation', *International Security*, vol. 40, no. 1, 2015, pp. 9–46, https://doi.org/10.1162/ISEC_a_00205.

94 Erez Manela, 'A Pox on Your Narrative: Writing Disease Control into Cold War History', *Diplomatic History*, vol. 34, no. 2, 2010, pp. 299–323.

95 Goldman Sachs, 'The US Is Poised for an Energy Revolution', 17 April 2023, https://www.goldmansachs.com/intelligence/pages/the-us-is-poised-for-an-energy-revolution.html.

96 Thomas Hobbes, in William Molesworth (ed.), *The English Works of Thomas Hobbes* (London: John Bohn, 1839), vol. III, 154. The full title of the 1651 publication was *Leviathan or The Matter, Forme, and Power of a Common-wealth Ecclesiasticall and Civil*.

97 Parker, *Global Crisis: War, Climate Change and Catastrophe in the Seventeenth Century*, Part I: 'The Placenta of the Crisis'.

JOURNAL SUBSCRIPTION INFORMATION

Six issues per year of the *Adelphi* Series (Print ISSN 1944-5571, Online ISSN 1944-558X) are published by Taylor & Francis Group, 4 Park Square, Milton Park, Abingdon, Oxon, OX14 4RN, UK.

Send address changes to Taylor & Francis Customer Services, Informa UK Ltd., Sheepen Place, Colchester, Essex CO3 3LP, UK.

Subscription records are maintained at Taylor & Francis Group, 4 Park Square, Milton Park, Abingdon, OX14 4RN, UK.

Subscription information: For more information and subscription rates, please see tandfonline.com/pricing/journal/tadl). Taylor & Francis journals are available in a range of different packages, designed to suit every library's needs and budget. This journal is available for institutional subscriptions with online only or print & online options. This journal may also be available as part of our libraries, subject collections, or archives. For more information on our sales packages, please visit: librarianresources.taylorandfrancis.com.

For support with any institutional subscription, please visit help.tandfonline.com or email our dedicated team at subscriptions@tandf.co.uk.

Subscriptions purchased at the personal rate are strictly for personal, non-commercial use only. The reselling of personal subscriptions is prohibited. Personal subscriptions must be purchased with a personal check, credit card, or BAC/wire transfer. Proof of personal status may be requested.

Back issues: Taylor & Francis Group retains a current and one-year back issue stock of journals. Older volumes are held by our official stockists to whom all orders and enquiries should be addressed: Periodicals Service Company, 351 Fairview Ave., Suite 300, Hudson, NY 12534, USA. Tel: +1 518 537 4700; email: psc@periodicals.com.

Ordering information: To subscribe to the Journal, please contact: T&F Customer Services, Informa UK Ltd, Sheepen Place, Colchester, Essex, CO3 3LP, United Kingdom. Tel: +44 (0) 20 8052 2030; email: subscriptions@tandf.co.uk.

Taylor & Francis journals are priced in USD, GBP and EUR (as well as AUD and CAD for a limited number of journals). All subscriptions are charged depending on where the end customer is based. If you are unsure which rate applies to you, please contact Customer Services. All subscriptions are payable in advance and all rates include postage. We are required to charge applicable VAT/GST on all print and online combination subscriptions, in addition to our online only journals. Subscriptions are entered on an annual basis, i.e., January to December. Payment may be made by sterling check, dollar check, euro check, international money order, National Giro or credit cards (Amex, Visa and Mastercard).

Printed in the United States
by Baker & Taylor Publisher Services